the VINTAGE TEA PARTY year

Angel Adoree

MITCHELL BEAZLEY

To the magnificent people in my life that fill me with love, hope, support, and inspiration. THANK YOU X

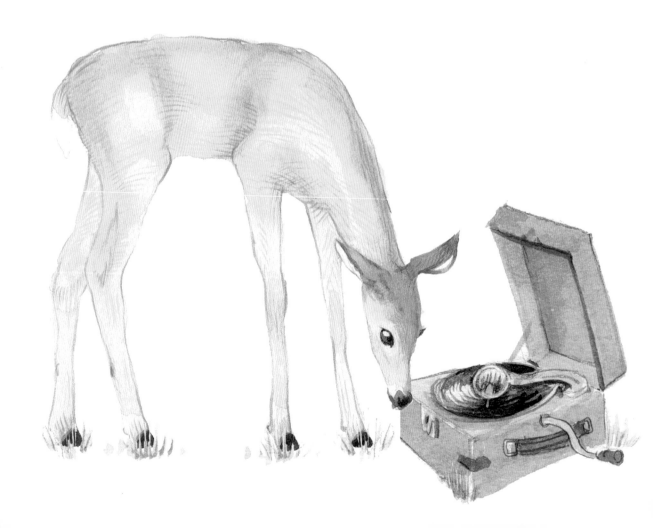

The Vintage Tea Party Year

by Angel Adoree

First published in Great Britain in 2012 by Mitchell Beazley,
an imprint of Octopus Publishing Group Limited,
Endeavour House, 189 Shaftesbury Avenue, London WC2H 8JY
www.octopusbooks.co.uk

An Hachette UK Company | www.hachette.co.uk

Distributed in the US by Hachette Book Group USA,
237 Park Avenue, New York, NY 10017, USA

Distributed in Canada by Canadian Manda Group,
165 Dufferin Street, Toronto, Ontario, Canada M6K 3H6

www.octopusbooksusa.com

Commissioning Editor Eleanor Maxfield | **Deputy Art Director & Designer** Yasia Williams-Leedham | **Senior Editor** Leanne Bryan | **Creative Director** Angel Adoree | **Photographers** Yuki Sugiura (food & drink); David Edwards (projects & locations) | **Illustrator** Adele Mildred

Hirani | **Proofreader** Jo Richardson | **Indexer** Isobel McLean | **Senior Production Controller** Caroline Alberti |

Home Economist Laura Fyfe | **Assistant Home Economist** Maura Cook | **Head of Craft** Sarah Keen | **Hair & Makeup** Sophia Hunt | **Copy Editor** Salima

Set in Reminga, Gorey, Justlefthand, and Lady Rene.

Printed and bound in China.

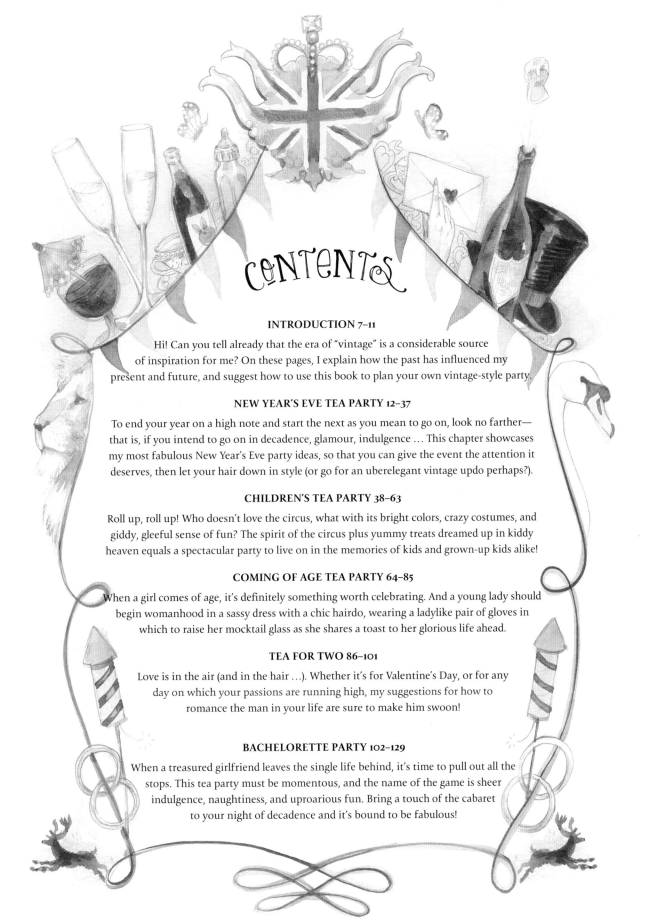

CONTENTS

INTRODUCTION

Welcome to *The Vintage Tea Party Year*. You are about to embark on a singular journey with me as I share and celebrate my passion for all things vintage. The following pages are inspired by the miracle of what Mother Nature has bestowed upon us through her four seasons, and I hope that they will, in turn, inspire your perfect tea party.

This book is divided into 12 chapters, which loosely represent a calendar year. I run a business that turns tea-party dreams into reality, offering people a little escapism from today's hectic life by transporting them to a time when life was simpler, yet steeped in glamour and decadence. I use the term "tea party" loosely—for me, instead of an afternoon treat taken between lunch and dinner, the phrase has evolved over the years into a style reference for the type of parties my company masterminds, and the demand for vintage-style tea parties of all shapes and sizes is now bigger than ever. In fact, this book has been inspired by you! With a few expert tips, there's no reason why you can't do the same just as successfully. To organize the perfect vintage tea party, you must:

1 Know your occasion—often they are chosen for us—wedding, bachelorette party, Christmas. But there are times when you get to choose, too! Why not throw a tea party simply because you can?!

2 Use this book to help you select the best foods, drinks, and decor for your event—each of the 12 chapters is based on a specific type of occasion. Use the appropriate chapter for inspiration, but there's no need to stick religiously to ideas from, say, the New Year's Eve chapter if you're planning a New Year's Eve party—mix and match recipes, craft projects, and hairstyles to suit your tastes.

3 Complement or expand your event planning with recipes and tips from my first book, *The Vintage Tea Party Book* (shameless plug).

Then, all there is left to do is to eat, drink, love, laugh, and be armed and prepared in the kitchen, so that you can thoroughly enjoy your tea party and hold onto the memory of it forever.

A fantastic bachelorette party we hosted, with the love of my life, Mr. Strawbridge, 2010.

Hosting a fabulous Christmas party, 2011.

MY JOURNEY

I like old things. Old-fashion, one-of-a-kind, handpicked items charm me with their uniqueness and personality in a way that only something with history can.

My journey started at 13 years of age, when I began thrifting in local flea markets. People sold their old junk out of the back of their cars, and my heart would race whenever I found a jewel, which was often very cheap. I became more attached to some items than others, and learned that certain things could fetch a decent amount of money for an East London girl like me, so in my early 20s I became a hospitable vintage dealer. I established a regular event called the Angel-A Vintage Experience, where I sold my finds, but also fed and watered the public in order to create the ultimate shopping experience!

Hosting is in my blood. My warm, giving parents, whose pictures are shown here, are wonderful role models. When I was a child, they were always feeding people in our family home, which eventually led to them owning an incredibly special restaurant full of love and great British food.

In 2007, the Angel-A Vintage Experience came to an end, and it seemed the most natural thing in the world to follow my parents' example and change the direction of my business toward hosting. The Vintage Patisserie was born.

I'm incredibly blessed to have hosted so many memorable events, from weddings, bar mitzvahs, and birthday parties for all ages to bachelorette parties, baby showers, and even a very memorable tea for two in the back of my London taxi! Each event is unique, and I feel electrified by people's happiness. I hope this book gives you the tools you need to touch people in the same way for any event that life throws at you—there really is a vintage tea-party spread that can fit the bill, no matter what the occasion.

Above: Nan and Grandad,
serving in WWII, 1943.

Right: Great Grandfather
having a good time, 1951.

Below: My dad (center) playing the Mad Hatter in his school play, 1959.

Right: My 13-year-old dad at the bar my uncle made, 1963.

Above: Me as a baby, very happy to be holding an apple, 1978.

Above: Mom and Dad on their wedding day, 1969.

Below: My brother and me at Christmas, 1982.

Right: My mom, dad, and brother at a family wedding, 1976.

THE PRESENT

It has been quite a year for me and the Vintage Patisserie. After 12 years of working from a converted school house in East London (which doubled as my home), we have moved to a fabulously quirky space just down the road in Hackney, where we now host the majority of our events. On a personal level, I've spent the year being quite sickeningly in love! (You'll notice the odd mention of the man himself in these pages.) I've learned how to balance this love with the rest of my life as a friend, daughter, and boss, and have watched my company grow and blossom.

When my first book, *The Vintage Tea Party Book*, was released last year, I felt incredibly nervous! My life's work was suddenly available to the public to critique, but I was blown away by the amazing response it received and I still pinch myself every day to make sure I'm not dreaming! My friends, family, and publisher all felt incredibly proud when it made it to a short list in the food and drink category at the National Book Awards in 2011—a truly magical night that I will never forget!

I've also spent the year crafting and styling this new book. Each recipe is lovingly tested and tasted, and each image has its own unique story and mood and is brought to life with vintage props, kitchenalia, and clothes. And I have met some truly wonderful people while working on the book, from Jon, the exclown who showed me around his circus and introduced to me to his wife, a former acrobat, to the excitable bunch of young ladies I took shopping for vintage-style outfits for the Coming of Age chapter. This book was put together with love and I hope this shows on every page.

Left: Gizzi Erskine and me at the launch of my first book, 2011.

Below: The Vintage Patisserie ladies hosting an Urban tea party at the flagship Puma store, 2012.

Above: Me, Zandra Rhodes, and my right-hand lady, Lauren, 2011. (I wore a vintage Zandra Rhodes dress on the cover of book 1, so it was a total honor to host a party for her!)

FOOD & DRINK BOOK OF THE YEAR

Left: Me at the Galaxy Book Awards, 2011.

Right: Dick, Lottie (who models in our Coming of Age chapter), and me, 2012.

Below: My family and me at our Street Party, 2012.

YOUR JOURNEY

Throwing a fabulous party is about creating a vision and bringing it to life. When you start to plan a party, you embark on your own unique journey, and when the guests begin to arrive, you take them along for the ride, too! This book is here for inspiration. But if you and I were sharing a pot of tea and a chat, and you asked if I had any tips to ensure your party goes with a big bang, this is what I would say:

"**Always start your journey with an invitation.** It will set the mood for the party and spark the excitement from the moment the envelope is opened! At the beginning of each chapter, you will find a prepared invitation. Feel free to photocopy it and use it as your own, or download it from *www.vintagepatisserie.co.uk*.

Plan your menu with price, production, and serving capability in mind. Do you have the right pots, plates, and so on? If not, get down to your local thrift shop! A spectacular tea party can be achieved on any budget.

Do something personal for your guests. It'll be the one memory that will stay with them always.

Be sure you are fully prepared. This means you'll be able to spend party time with your loved ones instead of just in the kitchen!

Finish with a thank you. It ends the journey with style and warmth and makes a great final page in your photo album! Photocopy the prepared thank you cards at the beginning of each chapter and use them as your own, or download them from *www.vintagepatisserie.co.uk*."

On that note, thank you for coming on this journey with me, and I raise my teacup to you:

"To your perfect tea-party year. May it bring health and happiness to you and all those you get drunk with—I mean, that you host!"

Love Angel ♥

The 31st of December is an incredibly important day in the calendar year. For me, it's often my only downtime, so I've made it totally mine to spend with my loved ones and spoil them rotten. On New Year's Eve, I love to reflect on the year gone by and to set my goals and intentions for the year ahead. There is no better way of celebrating the past and the future than by living in the now and basking in a glittering evening of glamour and decadence. Start as you mean to go on? I wish!

Happy New Year

Good Luck in the New Year!

Pigeon is a wonderful meat: it has hardly any fat and is full of gamey flavor. Cooked with woody mushrooms in a sweet red wine sauce, this light pithivier is divine. By the way, pithivier is just a fancy name for pie. It's New Year, after all, so I can't serve pie! If your man won't go out and shoot pigeon, store-bought duck is a great alternative. For non meat eaters, the pithivier is a great cooking platform for anything, including desserts.

MAKES 6

PREP 25 mins, plus marinating

COOK 40 mins

WILD MUSHROOM & PIGEON BREAST PITHIVIERS

6 pigeon breasts (about 9 ounces total weight), shot removed

1¾ pounds ready-to-bake puff pastry, thawed if frozen

all-purpose flour, for dusting

1 tablespoon olive oil

8 ounces wild mushrooms, sliced

2 tablespoons butter

2 garlic cloves, finely chopped

1 egg, beaten

For the marinade

1 garlic clove, crushed

leaves from 3 sprigs of thyme

6 black peppercorns, crushed

3 tablespoons extra-virgin olive oil

For the red wine sauce

2 tablespoons granulated sugar

1 cup red wine

2 sprigs of thyme

6 juniper berries, lightly crushed

salt and black pepper

1 For the marinade, combine the garlic, thyme leaves, peppercorns, and olive oil in a small bowl. Using a sharp knife, score the skin of the pigeon breasts lightly and rub in the marinade. Marinate in the refrigerator for at least 20 minutes.

2 Meanwhile, preheat the oven to 350°F. Roll out the pastry on a floured surface to a thickness of ¹/8 inch. Cut out twelve 4-inch circles.

3 Heat the olive oil in a skillet set over medium-high heat. Sauté the mushrooms for 5 minutes, then add the butter and garlic and cook for another 2 minutes. Transfer to a strainer set over a bowl to let any juices drain out. Put the skillet back on the stove, increase the heat, and sear the pigeon breast skin for 1½ minutes on each side to brown, then set aside for 5 minutes to rest.

4 Place a few mushrooms in the centers of 6 of the pastry circles.

Trim the breasts so that they sit inside a circle that has a diameter of about 2¾ inches—use a pastry cutter as a guide. Top with more of the mushrooms, brush around the edges with the beaten egg, and cover with the remaining pastry circles. Seal by lightly crimping the edges and decorate with spiral lines drawn with the point of a knife from the center outward.

5 Glaze the pastry with the egg wash and bake for 25 minutes or until golden brown.

6 Meanwhile, to make the red wine sauce, combine the sugar and a few drops of water in a small, clean saucepan set over high heat. Once the sugar melts and has become a dark golden brown, pour in the red wine. Add the thyme and the juniper berries. Cook the sauce for about 12–15 minutes, until it is reduced by two-thirds. Season to taste, strain, and serve warm alongside the pithiviers.

70
retti

I once heard that the chartreuse took its name from the Carthusian order of monks, who were vegetarians. The story states that the monks would hide forbidden meat in the center of the dish, enabling them to indulge. Naughty! It's a stunning dish that is incredibly satisfying to make. I will only make this on special occasions, and love doing so on New Year's Eve, while reflecting on my year and getting excited about what's ahead.

MINI CHARTREUSE of VEGETABLES

MAKES 6

PREP 30 mins, plus chilling

COOK 17–22 mins

¼ cup heavy cream

3 russet or Yukon gold potatoes, peeled, boiled, and well drained

salt and black pepper

½ butternut squash, peeled, boiled and well drained

3 large carrots, cut into sticks

3 cups fine green beans or asparagus tips, trimmed

8 Brussels sprouts, trimmed and leaves separated

½ cup peas

butter, for greasing

1 cup shredded sharp cheddar cheese

1 Add half the cream to the cooked and drained potatoes and mash them until smooth, seasoning to taste. Do the same for the butternut squash. The two mashed vegetables should feel quite stiff.

2 Trim the carrot sticks and beans or asparagus to fit the height of a ½-cup capacity ramekin. Parboil all the vegetables separately for about 2 minutes. Drain and rinse under cold water, then let dry.

3 Place a circle of nonstick parchment paper in the bottom of each of 6 ramekins and butter the sides thickly—don't skimp with the butter at this stage! Arrange the carrots and beans or asparagus alternately around the edge. Add enough peas to cover the bottom of each dish. Now layer up the potatoes, Brussels sprouts, cheese, and squash until you reach the top of the ramekin. Place the ramekins in the refrigerator for about 20 minutes to let the butter become firm. Preheat the oven to 350°F.

4 Place the ramekins on a baking sheet and bake for 15–20 minutes, then remove them from the oven and let set for 3–5 minutes before inverting onto serving dishes. If necessary, loosen the sides of the chartreuse from the ramekins with a sharp knife before turning out.

Your guests may not want to eat this dish for fear of ruining its elegant beauty. But an exciting journey begins the moment their taste buds experience the luxurious textures and flavor of the ballettes, and they will taste all the love and hard work you put into getting them to the table. Be warned: These are such a force for indulgence, your guests may end up jumping fully clothed into a bath full of Champagne, screaming "Happy New Year!"

Fois Gras Ballettes

MAKES 6

PREP 1 hour, plus cooling and chilling

COOK 11–15 mins

1 cup chicken consommé or chicken broth

1¾ tablespoons plain powdered gelatin

4 ounces foie gras (or faux gras—*see* note, below)

2 bunches watercress (about 4 ounces), to serve

For the egg garnish

4 eggs, separated

2½ tablespoons heavy cream

salt

butter, for greasing

red food coloring

1 In a small saucepan, pour the chicken consommé or broth over the gelatin and let sit for 5 minutes. Set the pan over low heat until the gelatin dissolves; do not let it boil. Take the pan off the heat and set aside to let the contents cool to room temperature.

2 To make the white egg garnish, mix the egg whites with 1 tablespoon of the cream and a pinch of salt. Beat the mixture well, then pour into greased dariole molds (we used 3 molds with 2½-inch bottoms). You want only a thin layer in each mold. Put about 2 inches boiling water in a saucepan, add the molds, making sure no water can enter them, and poach for 3–5 minutes, until firm. Turn it out to cool and, when cold, cut or stamp out the mixture in fancy shapes (we used star-shape cutters).

3 To make the pink egg garnish, mix 3 egg yolks with the remaining 1½ tablespoons cream and a pinch of salt. Add a few drops of food coloring to make the mixture turn light pink and beat well. Mold and poach the mixture as you did with the white egg garnish. Turn it out to cool, then cut or stamp out fancy shapes.

4 Pour some of the gelatin mixture (aspic gelatin) into 6 half-sphere molds, each with a diameter of 2½ inches, and swirl it around to cover the interior. This will hold the garnish in place. Using the shaped egg garnish, decorate around the sides of the molds. Let set in the refrigerator for 20 minutes.

5 Place a tablespoon of fois gras in the center of each mold to add another layer. Arrange some egg garnish over this, top with another layer of liquid aspic gelatin to fill the mold, then chill for 20 minutes, until firm.

6 Dip each mold into hot water and turn out the ballettes onto a bed of watercress to serve.

Note To avoid using foie gras, make "faux gras." Mellow some duck or chicken livers by soaking them overnight in milk with some garlic, thyme, salt, and black pepper. Dry the livers, sear them in a hot saucepan for 2 minutes (the centers should still be pink), then process with half their weight of soft butter until smooth. Adjust the seasoning and chill until set. This faux gras is silky smooth.

A few dishes that I passionately adore live in my "only-for-highly-momentous-occasions" category. One such occasion is Mother's Day, a special business achievement would be another, and New Year's Eve is the last. Rationing this particular delicacy allows me to appreciate the flavor of the sea all over again each time I get to taste it. Lobster Bisque is a classic French dish that celebrates the lobster by cooking it in its shell to extract and deepen every last morsel of flavor. It's a dish that will impress and, as long as you don't overcook the lobster, you can't go wrong!

Lobster Bisque

1 medium lobster

2 tablespoons butter

1 onion, finely chopped

4 garlic cloves, crushed

½ cup white wine

4 teaspoons Worcestershire sauce

2 teaspoons Tabasco sauce

½ teaspoon dried thyme

¼ cup brandy

2 cups hot water

2 cups whole milk

2 teaspoons smoked sweet paprika

¼ cup tomato paste

4 bay leaves

¼ cup white long-grain rice

2 cups heavy cream,
plus extra to serve (optional)

salt and black pepper

1 Remove the flesh from the lobster shell (or ask your fish dealer to do this for you), chop the lobster shell into large pieces, and set the meat aside. In a large saucepan, heat the butter over low heat and cook the lobster shells and the onion for about 7 minutes, until soft and translucent. Add the garlic and cook for about another 2 minutes.

2 Increase the heat to high and add the white wine to the pan. Cook the wine for about 1 minute, at the same time dislodging all the tasty sediment in the pan so that it combines with the mixture.

3 Add the Worcestershire and Tabasco sauces and the thyme and sauté for another minute, then add the brandy and stir.

4 Add the hot water, milk, paprika, tomato paste, and bay leaves and stir well.

5 Next, add the rice and let the mixture come to a gentle boil. Simmer for about 25 minutes, or according to the package directions, until the rice is cooked.

6 Remove the lobster shells and bay leaves and discard them. Puree the soup using a handheld immersion blender, or by passing it through a strainer, pushing the mixture through the mesh to puree it.

7 When the mixture is smooth and velvety, return it to the pan and set it over low heat. Add the lobster meat and cook gently until the soup is heated through. Then whisk in the cream, if using, and simmer just until the soup is warmed through; don't let it come to a boil.

8 Add salt and black pepper to taste. If desired, add a blob of cream in the middle of the soup bowl and swirl to serve.

HOW TO COOK YOUR LOBSTER

WHAT IF YOUR LOBSTER IS STILL SWIMMING?
The firm white meat of lobster is sweet and succulent. It's available all year round and it is widely agreed that lobster from colder waters has the best flavor. There are three main types. The best flavored is the European lobster, from around Britain, Ireland, Northern France, and Scandinavia. Then there is the American or Canadian; these have round, very fleshy claws. Finally, the slipper or squat lobsters live in warmer oceans, such as those surrounding Australia.

Before they are cooked, lobsters are very dark in color and range from blue/green to red/purple. However, when they are cooked, they turn a distinctive bright red color.

CHOOSING YOUR LOBSTER
The lobster that's easiest to use is store-bought, freshly cooked, split in half, and already cleaned. If you have a choice, go for the one with the brightest-colored shell, and that has the tail curled under the body (when cooked alive, the tails curl under).

For the freshest meat, buy a whole live lobster. Obviously, you need to choose the liveliest you can find, and its tail should definitely curl back under if you straighten it out. A frisky lobster is a fresh lobster.

A little care is necessary when handling lobsters: the plates on the tail move across each other when the tail opens and closes and the claws are seriously sharp and should be secured with rubber bands.

EXTRACTING THE FLESH
If you buy the lobster halved and freshly cooked, it's ready to eat. You may need to crack open the claws using a hammer, a pair of lobster crackers, or the back of a heavy chef's knife to get at the meat.

Live lobsters should be killed before cooking. The most humane way to kill your lobster is to put it into the freezer for a couple of hours, rendering it unconscious. Wrap it in a dish towel so that it can't move, then push the tip of a large, sharp knife through the center of its head (there is a cross shape on the head that marks the spot) about ¾–1¼ inches behind the eyes.

Put the lobster into a large saucepan of salted cold water and slowly bring it to a boil. When the water has reached boiling point, reduce the heat and simmer the lobster for about 15 minutes for the first 1 pound. Simmer for another 10 minutes for each extra 1 pound, for up to a maximum of 40 minutes. When the lobster is cooked, its shell will turn a deep brick red. Drain off the water and let the lobster cool.

To get the flesh out, first twist off the claws, then break into sections, crack the claw shell, and remove the flesh. Twist off the legs from the body, flatten with the back of a knife, and then use a pick or a teaspoon handle to remove the flesh.

Now sort out the body. To split the lobster in half along its length, insert a large, sharp knife and press down firmly. The body and tail should split lengthwise. Then cut through the head in the same way. You should now be able to separate the two halves. Remove and discard the pale stomach sac, the gills, and the dark intestinal thread along the length of the tail. The green pasty stuff in the body (or the "tomalley"), which is both its liver and pancreas, is considered a delicacy. Remove the tail meat and scrape out the soft flesh from the shell.

There may be coral-colored roe present. Mix this with butter to make lobster butter, which is wonderful on toast or added to sauces. Use leftover shells for stock.

These choux-pastry beauties are my secret weapons for showing off! The butterscotch is also a real treat. Did you know that swans are sometimes monogamous for their whole lives? I am so romanced by this idea! It really gets me in the mood for that magical midnight moment when I must kiss the first person I see ... Pucker up!

CHOUX PASTRY SWANS

MAKES 6

PREP 45 mins, plus cooling

COOK 25 mins

2 tablespoons butter, plus extra for greasing

½ cup white bread flour

1 teaspoon superfine sugar or granulated sugar

2 eggs, beaten

⅔ cup heavy cream

For the butterscotch sauce

4 tablespoons butter

¼ cup firmly packed dark brown sugar

¼ cup light corn syrup

1 tbsp lemon juice

⅓ cup heavy cream

edible gold luster spray (available online, optional)

1 Preheat the oven to 350°F.

2 To make the choux pastry, melt the butter in ⅔ cup water in a small saucepan over medium heat and bring to a full boil. Immediately add all the flour and sugar and stir continuously with a wooden spoon for a couple of minutes until the mixture pulls away from the side of the pan, forming a ball. Take the pan off the heat and continue stirring for 1 minute while the mixture cools.

3 Add the eggs, one by one, mixing the dough well to make sure each egg is thoroughly incorporated before adding the next. The dough should be smooth and glossy.

4 To make the swan bodies, spoon the dough into a pastry bag fitted with a plain medium tip. Pipe six mounds, each the equivalent of a tablespoon of the dough, onto a greased baking sheet, set about 3¼ inches apart.

5 Flatten each mound slightly with a fork dipped in water. Bake for about 15 minutes, until the choux puffs are golden brown and sound hollow when tapped. Cool on a wire rack.

6 To make the swan heads and necks, fit a pastry bag with a small plain tip and pipe S shapes, each about 2 inches long, onto a lightly greased baking sheet. Pinch the beginning of each "S" to make a beak. Bake for about 8 minutes until the choux puffs are golden brown. Be careful to avoid burning them. Cool on a wire rack.

7 Using an electric mixer, whip the cream until firm peaks form. Set aside in the refrigerator.

8 For the wings, slice off the top of each body with a serrated knife. Cut the tops in half lengthwise. Set aside.

9 Pipe the cream into the cavity of each choux puff, finishing about 2 inches above the top of the pastry.

10 Insert two wings, rounded edges down, into the center of each filling so that they form a V shape. Insert the S-shape neck into the cream.

11 To make the sauce, put the butter, sugar, and syrup into a saucepan and bring to a gentle simmer. Take the pan off the heat, add the lemon juice, and stir. Stir in the cream. To give the sauce a glittery shimmer, spray it with gold luster when in situ on a serving platter.

Do you remember the part in Alice in Wonderland where Alice meets the Queen of Hearts? There is an explosion of dancing cards, just before the sentence of "Off with her head." Well, this tart reminds me of that crazy scene. It is perfect for celebrating a special occasion and will make your guests want to dive in. And while it looks highly indulgent, it is actually incredibly refreshing to the palate after a lot of rich savory food.

Queen of Hearts Tart

For the pastry dough

4 cups all-purpose flour, plus extra for dusting

¾ cup confectioners' sugar

2 sticks butter, chilled and cubed

2 eggs, beaten

splash of milk (optional)

edible gold luster spray (available online, optional)

For the raspberry gelatin

2 sheets gelatin

4 cups frozen raspberries

2½ tablespoons superfine sugar or granulated sugar

SERVES **12**

PREP **30** mins, plus chilling

COOK **25** mins

1 Sift the flour and confectioners' sugar into a bowl. Rub in the butter. When the mixture resembles bread crumbs, mix in the eggs, adding some milk if the dough still looks dry. Bring the dough together into a ball with your hands. Wrap it in plastic wrap and chill for 30 minutes.

2 Preheat the oven to 340°F. Roll out the dough on a lightly floured surface and use it to line a 9-inch, loose-bottom fluted tart pan. Use pastry cutters to cut out heart and diamond shapes from the remaining dough. Put these on a baking sheet. Cover the tart shell with nonstick parchment paper and fill with pie weights or dried beans. Bake the shapes and tart shell for 15 minutes, then remove from the oven. Remove the paper and weights from the tart shell

and bake the shell for another 5 minutes. Let cool. Spray the pastry shapes with gold luster, if using, once cool.

3 To make the gelatin, cover the gelatin sheets with a little cold water and soak until softened. Put the raspberries, sugar, and 4 cups water in a saucepan. Heat the mixture gently until the sugar has dissolved, then simmer for a couple of minutes. Push it through a strainer into a clean saucepan, heat a little, then add the gelatin sheets (squeezing out the excess water) and let stand until dissolved. Strain into a small bowl and let cool.

4 Pour the gelatin into the tart, refrigerate for 3 hours, and top with shapes to serve.

At all momentous occasions, I would expect every guest to have something to take home with them to eat the next day. (No one would dream of not having a wedding cake, right?) So this is my New Year's version. Using festive flavors that are light after an indulgent evening, this bundt is not only a show-stopper to look at, but delicious, too.

CLEMENTINE & COINTREAU SYRUP BUNDT CAKE

SERVES 16

PREP 20 mins, plus cooling

COOK 1 hour–1 hour 20 mins

3⅛ sticks unsalted butter, softened, plus extra for greasing

2¼ cups granulated sugar

6 extra-large eggs, lightly beaten

grated rind of 6 clementines

4 cups all-purpose flour, plus extra for dusting

4 teaspoons baking powder

½ cup clementine juice

edible gold luster spray (available online, optional)

For the syrup

thin strips of rind (no pith) from 1 clementine

½ cup clementine juice

1⅔ cups confectioners' sugar

⅓ cup orange liqueur

1 Preheat oven to 350°F. Grease a large cathedral bundt cake mold (we used one that was 8¼ inches in diameter and 4 inches deep), lightly dust it with flour, and set it aside.

2 Cream the butter and sugar together with a wooden spoon or an electric mixer until light and fluffy, then slowly add the eggs and grated clementine rind, beating well after each addition. Fold in the flour, then the clementine juice, and spoon the batter into the prepared bundt pan.

3 Bake for 1 hour–1 hour 20 minutes, until a toothpick inserted into the middle comes out with just a few moist crumbs stuck to it. You may need to cover it after about 45 minutes of cooking to stop it from becoming too brown.

Set it on a wire rack to cool for 15 minutes, then turn out the cake and prick it all over with a toothpick.

4 While the cake is cooling, make the syrup. Place the strips of clementine rind and juice in a saucepan with the confectioners' sugar and heat gently until the sugar has completely dissolved.

5 Boil the syrup for 2–3 minutes, then remove from the heat and strain out the rind. Finally, add the orange liqueur. Spoon the syrup evenly over the cake. Let the bundt sit until the syrup has been absorbed, then spray it with edible gold luster, if using, to give it a shimmery finish.

Black bun is a traditional Scottish treat, originally reserved for Twelfth Night, but now served during the New Year festivities. It is actually a rich, moist fruitcake baked in a pastry crust. When it's made well, the fruit will stick to the knife when cut. Make this a few weeks before New Year's Eve so that the fruits absorb the alcohol and the cake matures to full flavor.

Traditional Black Bun

SERVES 10

PREP 25 mins, plus chilling and maturing

COOK 2 hours

1 egg, lightly beaten

about 2 tablespoons milk

For the pastry dough

1⅔ cups all-purpose flour, plus extra for dusting

½ teaspoon baking powder

pinch of salt

4 tablespoons butter, chilled and cubed

¼ cup vegetable shortening or lard, chilled and cubed

For the filling

1⅔ cups all-purpose flour

1⅓ cups raisins

1⅓ cups dried currants

1 cup slivered almonds

½ cup chopped candied peel

⅓ cup firmly packed dark brown sugar

2 tablespoons molasses

2 tablespoons brandy or whiskey, plus extra for brushing

1 teaspoon ground allspice

1 teaspoon ground cinnamon

1 teaspoon ground ginger

½ teaspoon black pepper

½ teaspoon baking soda

1 To make the dough, put the flour, baking powder, and salt in a bowl. Add the butter and shortening and rub with your fingertips until the mixture resembles bread crumbs. Stir in ¼ cup cold water and mix to a soft dough. Wrap in plastic wrap and chill it in the refrigerator while you make the filling.

2 Preheat the oven to 325°F. Mix together the filling ingredients with most of the beaten egg in a large bowl, adding enough milk to just moisten the mixture.

3 Dust a clean work surface with flour. Roll out three-quarters of the dough to a rectangle large enough to line the bottom and sides of a 9 × 5 × 3-inch loaf pan. Drape the dough into the pan and press it up against the sides, smoothing out any creases. Tightly pack in the filling and press it down well. Brush the top of the fruit mixture with some brandy or whiskey.

4 Roll out the remaining dough to a rectangle large enough to fit the top of the lined loaf pan. Dampen the edges of the dough in the loaf pan with water and press the dough lid on top,

then seal them well. Crimp the edges, if desired.

5 With a toothpick, make four holes through the top of the pastry, right down to the bottom of the pan, then use a fork to prick the surface all over. Brush the lid with the remaining beaten egg.

6 Bake for 2 hours. To prevent the top from browning too quickly, cover with aluminum foil or non-stick parchment paper toward the end of the cooking time. Let cool on a wire rack in the pan for 1 hour.

7 When cold, carefully turn out the bun onto foil. Use more foil to wrap it, then store it in an airtight container. Keep for at least 10 days in a cool, dry place before cutting the cake or it will fall apart.

New Year's Eve is the occasion for the biggest toast of the year. The entire world is celebrating together—how special is that? These are my favorite New Year tipples. They use traditional drinks you would expect to be served on such a momentous night, but also celebrate and mix in festive and seasonal ingredients. "Please raise your glass—may all your troubles during the coming year last only for as long as your New Year's resolutions!"

MULLED WHITE WINE SANGRIA

SERVES 6

PREP 25 mins, plus optional chilling

COOK 20–25 mins

½ cup honey, preferably orange blossom

rind of 2 lemons, cut into long strips

¼ cup freshly squeezed lemon juice

4 star anise

4 cinnamon sticks

12 cloves

2 bottles of dry white wine, such as Sauvignon Blanc

1 cup orange Muscat

1 apple, cored, halved, and thinly sliced

1 pear, cored, halved, and thinly sliced

2 lemons, thinly sliced crosswise

12 kumquats, thinly sliced crosswise

ice cubes (optional)

1 Bring 1 cup water, the honey, lemon rind and juice, star anise, cinnamon sticks, and cloves to a simmer in a large saucepan set over medium heat. Reduce the heat to low and cook for 15 minutes.

2 To serve cold, mix the spice mixture, wines, and fruit in a large pitcher. Cover and refrigerate overnight. Transfer the mixture to a large punch bowl and serve the drink with ice. To serve hot, heat the spice mixture and wines in a large saucepan over low heat until heated through. Add the fruit and divide among six mugs.

LEMON DROP CHAMPAGNE PUNCH

SERVES 6

PREP 20 mins, plus cooling

COOK 5 mins

3 lemons

½ cup superfine sugar or granulated sugar

1 bottle of Champagne, chilled

¾ cup best-quality vodka, chilled

1 Using a vegetable peeler, remove the rind from each lemon, working around the fruit in a long, continuous spiral. Juice the lemons and strain the pulp (you should have ¾ cup of juice). Set aside.

2 Heat the sugar with 1½ cup water in a small saucepan set over low heat, stirring until the sugar has dissolved. Bring the mixture to a boil, then take the pan off the heat. Add the lemon rind, then set the syrup aside for about 2 hours to cool completely.

3 Pour the Champagne, vodka, lemon juice, and syrup into a pitcher. Stir and pour the drink into a decanter or punch bowl.

COUNTDOWN COCKTAIL

¼ cup gin

⅓ cup blood orange juice

ice cubes

2 dashes of Angostura bitters

slice of blood orange, to garnish

SERVES 1

PREP 5 mins

1 Pour the gin and orange juice into an old-fashioned glass filled with ice cubes. Stir well.

2 Add the Angostura bitters and stir again. Decorate the drink with a slice of blood orange, then serve.

Lemon Drop Champagne Punch

Countdown Cocktail

Mulled White Wine Sangria

HOW TO CREATE
THE VICTORIANA

Make it your New Year's resolution to experiment and find the perfect vintage-look hairstyle for you. Here, I've taken inspiration from the Victorian era; think curled, coiffured hair and romantic updos. Believe it or not, this style is really easy to achieve. The most important thing is to first curl the hair tightly with as many curls as possible. If you need more volume, try adding a hair rat, or rat roll, which you can buy in pharmacies and online—or try making your own!

YOU WILL NEED

 hairspray curling tongs section clips tail comb bobby pins

 hair rat hairpins flowers and decorative hair barrettes

△ **STEP 1** Spray the hair with hairspray, then use the curling tongs to curl your hair into small, tight sections. Use the section clips to hold each curl while it cools. For this look, I used 3 curls around the hairline away from the face, 22 curls at the back, and 4 larger curls on top to create a soft wave.

△ **STEP 2** Once the curls have cooled, remove the clips but do not brush out the curls. Part the hair roughly through the center and, using bobby pins, secure the hair rat by pinning it at the bottom where it meets the head, and at the crown of the head.

△ **STEP 3** Tease the hair around the rat using a tail comb. Sweep it up in sections of various sizes to disguise the rat, and pin it in place. Once the rat is covered, pin the rest of the curls in place. Don't be too neat; this is a romantic look. Sweep the front away from your face and hide the ends in the curls around the rat.

◁ **STEP 4** To finish, add flowers, decorative hair barrettes—in fact, add whatever you want. This look should be completely over the top and playful!

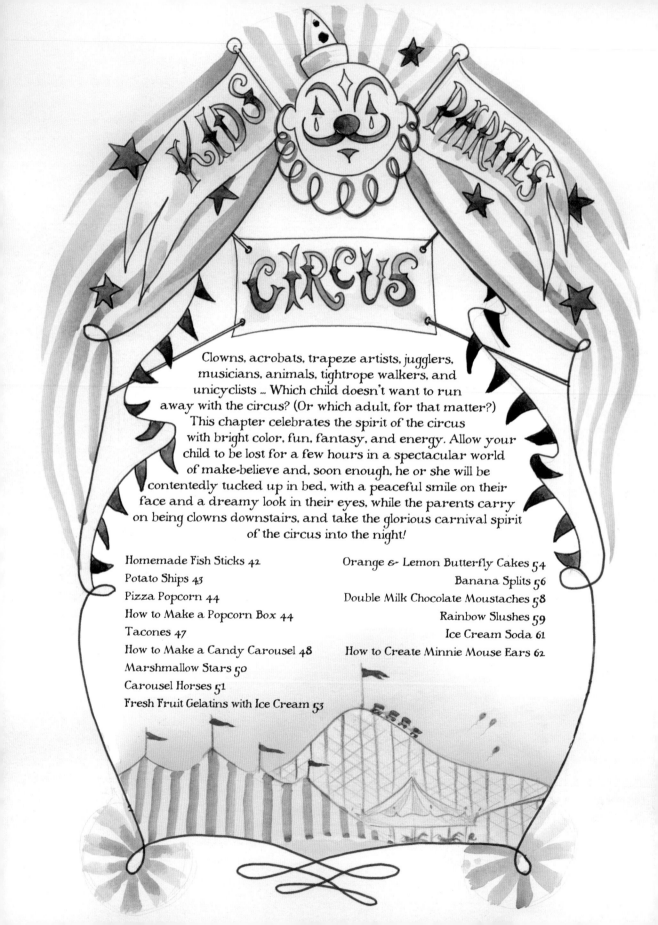

KIDS PARTIES

CIRCUS

Clowns, acrobats, trapeze artists, jugglers, musicians, animals, tightrope walkers, and unicyclists ... Which child doesn't want to run away with the circus? (Or which adult, for that matter?) This chapter celebrates the spirit of the circus with bright color, fun, fantasy, and energy. Allow your child to be lost for a few hours in a spectacular world of make-believe and, soon enough, he or she will be contentedly tucked up in bed, with a peaceful smile on their face and a dreamy look in their eyes, while the parents carry on being clowns downstairs, and take the glorious carnival spirit of the circus into the night!

Fish sticks and french fries was the meal of choice when my mom was pushed for time. I won't blame her for cooking store-bought but, cooked fresh, the crunch of bread crumbs with the flaky fish will be loved by all. Check out our cute custom-made cartons (*see page 44*), ideal for fish sticks with french fries.

HOMEMADE FISH STICKS

SERVES **6**

PREP **10** mins

COOK **20** mins

1 pound skinless sustainable white fish

1 egg

2 cups fresh white bread crumbs, made from day-old bread

rind and juice of 1 lemon

½ teaspoon dried oregano

salt and black pepper

3 tablespoons olive oil

ketchup, to serve

1 Preheat the oven to 350°F. Slice the fish into strips about ¾ inch wide and 3¼ inches long. Beat the egg in a small bowl. Tip the bread crumbs onto a plate and mix in the lemon rind along with the oregano and some salt and black pepper.

2 Gently heat the oil in a nonstick skillet. Working in batches, dip the fish strips into the egg, then roll them in the seasoned bread crumbs and cook for a minute or so on each side until golden. Transfer the fish to a baking sheet and bake for 10 minutes, until cooked through. Serve immediately with ketchup.

I believe the love of potatoes begins at birth, but I would feel guilty serving up a potato without the fun factor! When I saw these ships at a grown man's nautical-themed party, I just had to borrow the idea. Sail on with any topping of your choice.

SERVES **12**

PREP **15** mins

COOK **25–30** mins

POTATO SHIPS

12 small new potatoes

4 thin slices of ham

2 cherry tomatoes

½ cup shredded cheddar cheese

1 Preheat the oven to 400°F. Bake the potatoes on a baking sheet for 25–30 minutes. Meanwhile, cut the ham into little triangles. Quarter the cherry tomatoes, then halve widthwise. Skewer the ham and tomato pieces onto toothpicks, as shown in the picture, to make the sails.

2 Remove the potatoes from the oven and, when cool enough to handle, slice off the tops. Sprinkle with the cheese and place the sails on top. Serve immediately.

For a healthy yet tasty belly-filler, popcorn is the perfect snack. Add some delicious pizza-inspired spices, make a simple popcorn box with our circus-themed design (see below), and let the fun begin! Don't forget to individually label each box—kids will love to take these home with them to use again on a movie night.

PiZZa POPCORN

SERVES 6

PREP 10 mins

COOK 5 mins

2 tablespoons vegetable oil

1½ cups popping corn

2 tablespoons grated Parmesan cheese

1 teaspoon garlic powder

1 teaspoon dried Italian herb seasoning

½ teaspoon sweet paprika

½ teaspoon salt

1 Heat the oil in a large saucepan with a tight-fitting lid over medium heat. Add the popping corn, shake the kernels around to coat them in the oil, then place the lid on the pan and let heat on the stove, shaking it occasionally, until there is about a 2- or 3-second gap between each pop.

2 Meanwhile, combine the remaining ingredients in a large bowl. Remove the popcorn from the heat and toss it through the spices. Serve immediately, presented in personalized popcorn boxes.

HOW TO MAKE a POPCORN bOX

1 Photocopy the box template to the right, enlarging it to your desired size. Cut out the photocopy and glue it onto thin cardboard. Color in the design, then cut out the shape.

2 Score and fold along the lines as necessary, then fold the box into shape.

3 Glue the flaps on the inside of the box. Let dry.

4 Add some popcorn!

For added fun with a twist on the ice cream, these tacones are too cute for words, what with the tasty chicken, the crunch of the cone, and the fresh salad. Feel free to change the filling to suit your own tastes.

SERVES **12**

PREP **20** mins, plus marinating

COOK **10** mins

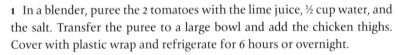

Tacones

2 tomatoes, coarsely chopped

juice of 1 lime

½ teaspoon salt

1 pound boneless, skinless chicken thighs

3 corn tortillas

1 tablespoon vegetable oil

½ teaspoon sweet paprika

½ teaspoon dried parsley

½ cup shredded cheddar cheese

For the salsa

½ avocado

½ onion

1 tomato

1 tablespoon chopped fresh cilantro

1 In a blender, puree the 2 tomatoes with the lime juice, ½ cup water, and the salt. Transfer the puree to a large bowl and add the chicken thighs. Cover with plastic wrap and refrigerate for 6 hours or overnight.

2 Preheat the oven to 400°F. Cut the tortillas into quarters and roll up each one to form a cone. Secure these with toothpicks, then place them on a baking sheet. Bake the cones for 5 minutes, then reshape the cones slightly, if necessary, before they cool. Place them on a wire rack, let cool, then remove the toothpicks.

3 Set the broiler to high. Remove the chicken thighs from the marinade, pat them dry, and place them on a broiler pan. Brush with the oil and sprinkle with the paprika and parsley. Broil them for 10 minutes on each side until the chicken is lightly charred and cooked through.

4 Meanwhile, make the salsa. Dice the avocado, onion, and tomato, then toss them all together with the chopped cilantro.

5 Transfer the chicken to your work surface and let stand for about 5 minutes. Cut the thighs into strips. Layer the chicken, cheese, and salsa upright in the cones to assemble the tacones.

HOW TO MAKE A CANDY CAROUSEL

I still remember my first time on a carousel and I've seen the film footage that my mom took of me sitting on my dad's lap with the biggest smile on my face many times. You can make this carousel to delight the children, and hang delicious treats for them from it, such as the Marshmallow Stars and Carousel Horses on pages 50 and 51, to pull off and eat.

YOU WILL NEED

✂ 1 side plate (for a template) ✂ 1 saucer with a diameter at least ½ inch smaller than your side plate (for a template) ✂ pen or pencil ✂ 24 × 16-inch white mounting board, 1/16 inch thick ✂ paper scissors ✂ string ✂ ruler ✂ cardboard tube from plastic wrap/aluminum foil—its length should be equal to the height of your pencils + 2½ inches ✂ glue gun ✂ colored paints (optional) ✂ 6–7 sheets 11 × 8½-inch paper in bright colors ✂ craft knife ✂ cutting mat ✂ bamboo skewers ✂ 1 yard colored ribbon, 1¼–1½ inches wide (optional) ✂ treats for threading ✂ 5 unused pencils of one length ✂ glue stick ✂ hack saw ✂ adhesive-backed paper (optional)

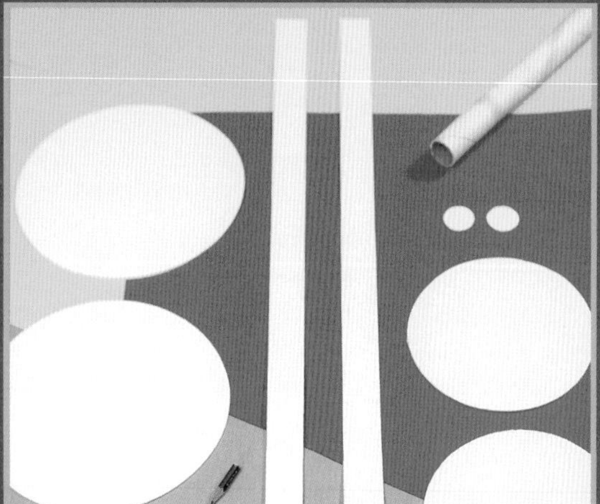

CUT OUT THE MOUNTING BOARD PIECES

1 Using your side plate and saucer as templates, draw and then cut out two larger circles and two smaller circles from the mounting board. Draw the circles close together, because you will need more mounting board in step 4.

2 Run the string around the circumference of one of your larger circles, then measure the piece of string to find the length of the circle's circumference.

3 Mark out two strips on the mounting board—each should be 1¼ inches wide, and the length should be the same as the circumference of the larger circle. Cut out the strips.

4 Draw around the end of your cardboard tube twice on the mounting board to make two small circles and cut them out. Use the glue gun to attach one circle to each end of your tube.

MAKE THE CAROUSEL CIRCLES

1 Glue the long edge of one of the strips around the bottom of one of the larger circles, gluing and holding as you work. Repeat with the other strip and larger circle.

2 Using the end of your tube as a template, cut a circle in the center of both smaller circles and one larger circle.

3 Start decorating—it is easier to do so before assembly. Paint the smaller circles or cover them with colored paper.

4 Take a smaller circle and, using the craft knife and cutting mat, make 4–6 small evenly spaced incisions ½ inch from the outer rim. Attach bamboo skewers for the treats. It's easier to thread the treats onto them first, then position them on the carousel. Pass each skewer through an incision and secure with glue where it passes through. Or cut 4–6 lengths of ribbon that are long enough to be looped, yet will hang from the top of the carousel at a good height for treats to be strung onto them. Pass the aligned ends of each loop through an incision and knot them to secure it in place.

MAKE THE CAROUSEL POLES

1 Cut long 1½-inch-wide strips of color paper and apply glue to them. Roll up a pencil in a strip of paper, slowly pushing out air bubbles as you work. Repeat with three of the remaining pencils. They will look slightly rectangular.

2 Cut a long 1¼-inch-wide strip from two sheets of colored paper. Apply glue to one side of the first strip. Wrap it around the cardboard tube, from the top down, in a barber-shop pole effect. Apply glue to the second color paper strip and wrap the tube with it in the same way, covering any gaps.

3 Carefully cut off the writing-end tip of the remaining pencil with a hack saw, about ¾–1¼ inches from the sharpened tip. This tip will become the pivot on which the carousel spins. Using the glue gun, attach the pivot to one end of your tube, with the sharpened tip facing down.

ASSEMBLE THE CAROUSEL

1 The larger circle without the hole will be the bottom of the carousel. Using your glue gun, attach the four covered pencils around the inside of the rim, spacing them evenly.

2 Hold the inner tube in place so that the pencil tip rests in the middle of the base. Push the two smaller circles onto the

inner tube, starting with the one without the ribbons. (These will hang from the upper smaller circle.) The circles should fit snugly around the tube without sliding down along it— the holes are just big enough for the tube to fit through.

3 Push the remaining larger circle onto the tube, leaving an inch or so protruding at the top for a handle. Reach inside the top rim and glue the ends of the pencils to the inside of it. The main body is now complete—it should be a solid structure and the pole in the center should spin on the pencil pivot when turned by the handle.

4 Now to make it look pretty! Be creative—we used paper and adhesive-backed paper to add color and pattern to our carousel. Use ribbon or paper and the glue gun to cover the handle and to add detail to the top of the carousel.

MARSHMALLOW STARS

MAKES **24**

PREP **25** mins, plus setting

COOK **15** mins

vegetable oil, for greasing

equal amount confectioner' sugar and cornstarch mixed together, for dusting

1¾ tablespoons plain powdered gelatin

1 cup granulated sugar

1 tablespoon liquid glucose

1 extra-large egg white

½ teaspoon vanilla extract

1 Lightly grease 24 silicone star-shape molds (about 1½ inches deep and 1½ inches wide) and dust with the confectioners' sugar-and-cornstarch mixture.

2 Place the gelatin in a bowl. Boil some water, let it stand for 30 seconds, then pour ⅓ cup water over the gelatin and stir until it has dissolved.

3 Put the granulated sugar, glucose, and 1 cup water into a heavy saucepan. Warm over low heat until the sugar dissolves, then increase the heat and boil until the temperature of the sugar syrup reaches 257°F on a candy thermometer. Take off the heat, pour it over the gelatin mixture, and mix well.

4 Beat the egg white in a large bowl with an electric mixer until stiff peaks form, then pour the hot sugar syrup from the pan over it in a slow, steady stream, beating all the time. The mixture will become shiny and start to thicken. Add the vanilla extract and continue beating for 5–10 minutes, until the mixture is stiff and thick. When you lift the beaters, a trail of the mixture should remain on the surface for 3 seconds.

5 Spoon the mixture into the prepared star molds and smooth with a wet spatula. Let set for at least 1 hour in a cool place (but not in the refrigerator).

6 Dust your work surface with more of the confectioners' sugar-and-cornstarch mixture. Loosen the marshmallows around the edges of each mold with a small knife, then turn them out onto the dusted surface. Decorate the marshmallows to your heart's content (try edible luster sprays, available online, or melted chocolate with any sprinkles you prefer), then add them to your candy carousel (*see pages 48–49*) if you want! Or store them in a lined airtight container, separating each marshmallow from the next with nonstick parchment paper.

CAROUSEL HORSES

1½ sticks unsalted butter, softened

3 tablespoons granulated sugar

1 teaspoon vanilla extract

grated rind of ½ lemon

2 egg yolks

1¾ cups all-purpose flour, plus extra for dusting

¼–¾ cup raspberry or strawberry preserves

MAKES 30
PREP 30 mins,
plus chilling and cooling
COOK 10 mins

1 Cream the butter and sugar together with a wooden spoon or an electric mixer until light and fluffy. Beat in the vanilla extract, lemon rind, and egg yolks, then finally mix in the flour.

2 Wrap the dough in plastic wrap and chill in the refrigerator for 30 minutes.

3 Preheat the oven to 350°F. Line three baking sheets with nonstick parchment paper.

4 Remove the dough from the refrigerator and place it on a lightly floured work surface. Roll out the dough to a thickness of about ¼ inch.

5 Cut 60 shapes from the dough using a horse-shape cookie cutter and place them on the prepared baking sheets. Using a toothpick, give each horse a hole in the top of its back and another where its eye would be.

6 Bake the dough shapes for 8–10 minutes, until pale golden. Remove the baking sheets from the oven and let them stand for a few minutes, then transfer the cookies to wire racks to cool.

7 When cool, spread ½–1 teaspoon of preserves on half the horses, leaving a ½-inch border around the edges. Top with the other halves so that the preserves poke through the eye holes.

8 Skewer through the holes on the horses' backs with toothpicks and arrange the horses on your candy carousel (*see* pages 48–49).

A party is not a party without gelatin and ice cream. Everyone knows this. Personally, I'm not a fan of store-bought flavored gelatin, but I love this fresh fruit gelatin. It's healthy, colorful, and even better when served in an old-fashion candy jar with a big dollop of ice cream!

FRESH FRUIT GELATINS WITH ICE CREAM

1 Place the gelatin in a saucepan and pour the juice over it. Let stand for 5–10 minutes.

2 Gently heat the saucepan over low heat until the gelatin has dissolved; do not let it boil.

3 Carefully pour the gelatin into candy jars, serving dishes, or decorative glasses, then place them in the refrigerator for at least 2 hours, until set. Serve with ice cream.

SERVES 6

PREP 20 mins,
plus setting

COOK 5 mins

1¾ tablespoons unflaovered powdered gelatin

2 cups fresh juice, such as orange, mango, or passion fruit (avoid pineapple, papaya, and kiwi, because they affect how the gelatin sets)

ice cream, to serve

I'm embarrassed to admit this, but my father and I have a secret competition every year at my Auntie's house to see who can hide the greatest number of her butterfly cakes so that we can smuggle them home at the end. I'm particularly embarrassed because I'm using the present tense! My Auntie's cakes are so yummy, and the entire family has loved them for as long as I can remember. These light and zesty bites are a real treat.

Orange & Lemon Butterfly Cakes

MAKES 20
PREP 20 mins
COOK 15 mins

For the cake

2 tablespoons unsalted butter, softened

½ cup granulated sugar

1 extra-large egg, beaten

¾ cup all-purpose flour

¾ teaspoon baking powder

grated rind of 1 orange

grated rind of 1 lemon

¼ cup milk

For the buttercream

1 stick unsalted butter, softened

¾ cup confectioners' sugar

1 Preheat the oven to 350°F. Line two 12-cup mini-muffin pans with 20 paper cupcake liners.

2 To make the cake, cream the butter and sugar together with a wooden spoon or an electric mixer until light and fluffy. While you are still beating, add the egg and continue beating until thoroughly mixed.

3 Beat in the flour and half the orange and lemon rind until just combined.

4 Beat in the milk and spoon the batter into the paper cupcake liners. Bake in the middle of the oven for 15 minutes or until golden and risen.

5 Remove from the oven and let cool in the pans on a wire rack.

6 To make the buttercream, beat together the butter, confectioners' sugar, and the remaining orange and lemon rind, using a wooden spoon or an electric mixer, until smooth and creamy.

7 When the cakes are cool, use a small serrated knife to carefully slice a small circle from the top of each cake. Cut each circle in half. Spoon a little buttercream on top of each cake, then gently replace the halved circles in a butterfly-wing position.

This is the perfect way to dress up a banana, and it's speedy, too! Cream plus semisweet chocolate equals deliciousness. The only thing you will have to decide is what the bananas will wear. Sprinkles, crushed pistachio nuts, grated white chocolate ... the list is endless.

BaNaNa SPLiTS

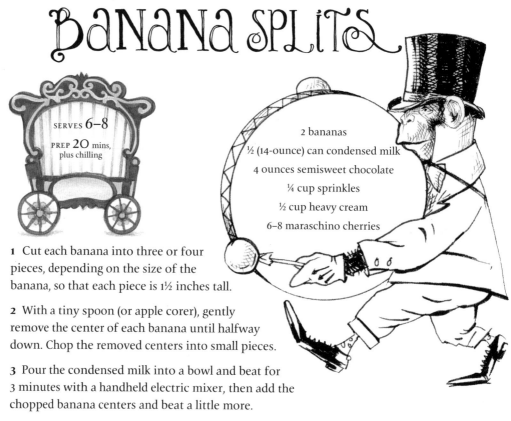

SERVES 6–8

PREP 20 mins, plus chilling

2 bananas
½ (14-ounce) can condensed milk
4 ounces semisweet chocolate
¼ cup sprinkles
½ cup heavy cream
6–8 maraschino cherries

1 Cut each banana into three or four pieces, depending on the size of the banana, so that each piece is 1½ inches tall.

2 With a tiny spoon (or apple corer), gently remove the center of each banana until halfway down. Chop the removed centers into small pieces.

3 Pour the condensed milk into a bowl and beat for 3 minutes with a handheld electric mixer, then add the chopped banana centers and beat a little more.

4 Break the chocolate into pieces and melt it in a heatproof bowl set over a saucepan of barely simmering water, making sure the bottom of the bowl doesn't touch the water below.

5 Pour the sprinkles onto a saucer. Dip the bottom of each banana piece into the melted chocolate, then roll the chocolatey parts in the sprinkles. Place the bananas, chocolate-end down, on some nonstick parchment paper, spoon the banana-and-condensed milk mixture into the centers, and let chill in the refrigerator for 1 hour.

6 Just before serving, whip up the cream and, using a star tip, pipe it on top of the bananas. Top each with a maraschino cherry.

I know a thing or two about moustaches. My dad had the best handlebar moustache in the 1970s and 80s, and my partner has the biggest moustache in show business (or so he tells me)! So my moustache-shape cookie cutters are treasured possessions.

Double MILK CHOCOLATE MOUSTACHES

MAKES **16**

PREP **25** mins, plus chilling

COOK **15–20** mins

1¾ sticks unsalted butter, softened

¾ cup granulated sugar

1 egg

2 cups all-purpose flour, plus extra for dusting

pinch of salt

2½ tablespoons unsweetened cocoa powder

½ cup milk chocolate chips, or a chocolate bar cut into small pieces

1 Preheat the oven to 350°5. Line a baking sheet with nonstick parchment paper.

2 Cream the butter and sugar together with a wooden spoon or an electric mixer until light and fluffy. Beat in the egg, then the flour, salt, and cocoa powder. Fold in the chocolate chips or pieces, then bring the dough together in a ball. Wrap it in plastic wrap and refrigerate for 20 minutes.

3 Roll out the dough on a lightly floured work surface to a thickness of ¼ inch. Carefully cut out 16 shapes using a moustache-shape cookie cutter (available online).

4 Place the dough shapes on the baking sheet and bake for 15–20 minutes. Remove from the oven and cool on a wire rack.

Is anything more beautiful than a rainbow, with its layers of rich color, one softly merging into the next? To have this visual delight in a teacup is a total treat, and a refreshing one that will light up any child's eyes and perk up their taste buds!

RAINBOW SLUSHES

MAKES 6

PREP 10 mins, plus freezing

12 ice pops of varying colors

1 Remove the ice pops from the freezer to defrost a little. When they are slushy, pour a layer into six freezerpoof glasses; put these in the freezer to set. Refrigerate the slushy ice pops until the first layer is frozen, then repeat the process until all the layers are frozen. Place the slushes in the freezer until ready to serve.

What can be better on a warm summer's day than something sweet, cool, and fizzy? There are no rules to devising your own combinations of soda and ice cream flavors—make them as wacky or conventional as you like. As a kid, I always had cola and vanilla ice cream. How do you float yours?

ice cream soda

MAKES **1**

PREP **1** min

1 cup soda of your choice (cola, lemon-flavored, or some other), chilled

1 scoop of ice cream

1 Pour the soda into a tall glass.

2 Top the soda with a scoop of ice cream and add a colorful straw.

TIP

Prepare ahead if serving ice cream sodas at a party. Line a baking sheet with nonstick parchment paper and place this in the freezer until cool. Remove the ice cream from the freezer and let it stand until slightly softened. Then remove the prepared baking sheet from the freezer and quickly place scoops of ice cream onto it so that the ice cream scoops don't melt. This will make things easier for you during a party, because all you need to do is to pour your sodas and simply pop the prepared scoops into the drinks. No struggling with rock-solid ice cream and an unwieldy ice cream scoop for the elegant hostess!

HOW TO CREATE
MINNIE MOUSE EARS

Minnie Mouse first shimmied onto the silver screen as Mickey Mouse's love interest in the 1928 movie *Steamboat Willie*. With her red polka dots and oversize bow and shoes, Minnie is a classic childhood style icon, and recreating her famous mouse ears couldn't be easier! This hairstyle will work well on all hair types, but, of course, it can't be done with hair that is any shorter than shoulder length, because short hair cannot be placed in a high bun.

YOU WILL NEED

hairbrush ~ 2 hairbands ~ tail comb ~ bristle brush ~ hairspray ~ hairpins ~ 2 ribbons tied in a bow, or a bow on a pin

◁ **STEP 1** Brush the hair and part it neatly into even ponytails, securing each with a hairband. Each ponytail should be positioned high on the head, where the "ears" will be.

◁ **STEP 2** Tease one ponytail with a tail comb, then gently smooth the surface of the hair with a bristle brush—be careful to avoid brushing out the volume you've just added. Now spray the ponytail with hairspray. Repeat with the other ponytail.

▷ **STEP 3** Holding the end of a ponytail, roll it forward loosely, turning the hair over toward the front of the head. Hold the roll in place with one hand and use the other to fan out the hair so that the two sides of the roll sit on the head on each side of the roll. Pin the roll in place, then repeat on the other side. Smooth flyaway strands with your hand and spray the rolls with hairspray.

◁ **STEP 4** For the finishing touch, pin a bow to the bottom of each bun or between them. It's worth remembering that later, when the party is over and you are brushing out teased hair, instead of starting near the scalp, you should always start at the ends of the hair and gradually work up the hairshaft.

The thirteenth birthday is pretty significant
for a young lady. It's a rite of passage into the next
stage of your blossoming life. Thirteen opens the doors to
experimentation—with makeup, cooking, and dressing up, and in
developing your passions—so it should be celebrated! My own obsession
with flea markets started at this age, which was considered odd for
someone so young. Whatever your passion, follow your heart and do
what you want to do—but do it well! You never know where it could lead...

When I was at school, I had several best friends, and as soon as I was home from a long day at school I would call them and chat to them for hours. My dad just could not understand what we had to talk about, having been together at school all day long and, looking back, I have no idea either! I always used to nibble on cheese and fruit while I was on the phone, and this recipe is an updated, more elegant version of that snack, using soft creamy goat cheese, rolled in anything you like.

Goat Cheese Truffles

MAKES 10

PREP 10 mins,
plus chilling

10–12 ounces goat cheese, chilled

Your choice of the following coatings (each yields enough mixture to coat about 10 truffles, depending on how thick you like your coating to be)

2 tablespoons chopped green herbs, such as chives, parsley or mint, plus a sprinkling of cracked black pepper

1 tablespoon smoked sweet paprika

2 tablespoons toasted sesame seeds

2 tablespoons poppy seeds

2 tablespoons chopped nuts, such as walnuts, pine nuts, or pistachio nuts

2 tablespoons finely chopped dried fruit, such as apricots

1 Line a baking sheet with nonstick parchment paper. Shape a small spoonful of goat cheese about the size of a walnut into a ball by rolling it between the palms of your hands. Place it on the prepared baking sheet. Repeat with the remaining cheese until you have 10 balls.

2 Put your chosen coatings on individual saucers and roll each truffle in the coating, making sure it is evenly coated, then place it on the prepared baking sheet.

3 Cover the truffles loosely with plastic wrap and chill them in the refrigerator for 20 minutes.

4 When you are ready to eat, pierce each truffle with a decorated toothpick (which makes it easier to pick up the truffles), then transfer them, one by one, onto a decorative serving dish.

I insisted that the theme of my coming-of-age party be mocktails and canapés because I wanted to be grown up, and had often seen my mum eat canapés at parties. My Rose Beef Bites are delicate and also delicious, with beef and horseradish being lifelong friends. Spending a tiny amount of time to be sure the beef looks pretty makes these canapés stunning to behold. Assemble the beef before the party, so then it's only a matter of spread, drop, serve, and smile!

ROSE BEEF BITES
WITH HORSERADISH CREAM

MAKES **18**
PREP **20** mins
COOK **7–10** mins

1 small baguette

2 tablespoons butter, melted

9 thin slices of rare roast beef

18 watercress leaves

For the horseradish cream

½ cup crème fraîche or sour cream

1 tablespoon grated horseradish

salt and black pepper

1 Preheat the oven to 350°F. Slice the baguette into 18 thin circles. Brush both sides of each slice with melted butter. Place the baguette circles on a baking sheet and toast them in the oven for about 7–10 minutes, turning halfway through, until brown, then let cool.

2 To make the horseradish cream, combine the crème fraîche or sour cream with the horseradish and season to taste. When the baguette circles have cooled, place a spoonful of horseradish cream on top of each one.

3 Cut each slice of beef in half lengthwise, then roll it up to form a pretty rose spiral. Place a roll of beef on top of each baguette circle, then garnish with watercress leaves.

At every party I threw during my teens, my mom made chicken on sticks. She knew it was foolproof. The chicken was sometimes flavored with barbecue sauce, sometimes with Mexican or Indian spices, and at other times it would be cooked on the barbecue with loads of vegetables. Below is my favorite variation; I loved the kick of the harissa, and the sweet pea and watercress soup is a fantastic complement. Serve the chicken on decorative toothpicks, which look incredibly feminine next to a teacup of soup.

STiCKY CHiCKEN SKEWERS WiTH PEA & WATERCRESS SOUP

SERVES **6**

PREP **35** mins, plus marinating and cooling

COOK **20** mins

For the skewers

1 tablespoon vegetable oil

1 teaspoon smoked sweet paprika

pinch of salt

1 skinless chicken breast, cut into thumbnail-size pieces

1 tomato, seeded and cut into thumbnail-size pieces

1 tablespoon harissa

For the soup

2 tablespoons butter

1 small onion, thinly sliced

3 bunches of watercress

2 cups chicken or vegetable stock or broth

3½ cups fresh peas

small bunch of chervil, finely chopped

1 To make the chicken skewers, mix together the oil, paprika, and salt in a bowl, then add the chicken, coating it well. Cover the bowl with plastic wrap and refrigerate for 30 minutes to marinate.

2 Heat a skillet over medium heat and sauté the chicken for 5–7 minutes, until cooked through, nudging it around to stop it from sticking to the skillet. Don't let it brown too much—it should remain moist. Set the chicken aside until it is cool enough to handle.

3 To assemble the skewers, thread the chicken and tomato pieces onto decorative toothpicks and sprinkle with the harissa.

4 To make the soup, melt the butter in a saucepan set over medium heat. Add the onion and cook for 5–7 minutes, until softened. Add the watercress and cook for another 2–3 minutes, until it wilts.

5 Add the stock, peas, and half the chervil. Bring to a boil, reduce the heat, and simmer for 3–4 minutes, until the peas are cooked.

6 To prevent the soup from overcooking, pour it into a large bowl and sit it in a bowl of ice cubes. Let the soup cool completely, then puree it in a food processor and pass it through a fine strainer. Stir in the remaining chervil and serve the soup with the chicken skewers.

My obsession with tarte tatin (an unside-down pie) will never end, and I hope that by the time I'm 100, I will have tarte tatined everything possible! This is my newest elegant take on a favorite after-school treat—an onion sandwich. My mom often cooked onions as the base of dishes, and the wonderful smell of buttery, salted onions was too much to take! We often shared a naughty onion sandwich while talking about our days. I'm sure she always cooked extra onions to compensate.

MAKES 6
PREP 25 mins
COOK 40 mins

SHaLLOT TaRTES TaTIN

5 shallots

2 tablespoons butter

1 teaspoon granulated sugar

1 teaspoon thyme leaves

2 bay leaves

1 tablespoon balsamic vinegar

½ cup red wine

salt and black pepper

1 sheet ready-to-bake puff pastry

all-purpose flour, for dusting

1 Remove the skins from the shallots and cut them into quarters lengthwise, cutting from the stem straight through the root.

2 Heat the butter and sugar in a heavy saucepan set over medium heat. When the butter begins to bubble, sprinkle with the thyme and bay leaves, then add the shallots. Cook for 5 minutes, stirring occasionally. Pour the balsamic vinegar and red wine over the shallots and season to taste. Reduce the heat and cook gently for 12–15 minutes.

3 Meanwhile, preheat the oven to 375°F. Roll out the pastry on a lightly floured work surface to a thickness of ¼ inch. Make sure that you roll it out so that it is large enough to cut into six 2¾-inch circles. Cut out the pastry circles using a pastry cutter.

4 Divide the shallots among six cups of a cupcake pan. Cover each with a disk of pastry and gently press it down around the edges. Bake the tarts for about 15–20 minutes, until golden and puffed up. Serve the tarts immediately.

This Italian delight is a great treat to add to your young lady's party. What could be better than a blend of almond, orange and chocolate? Biscotti are easy to eat, simple to prepare, and can be made up to two weeks in advance. Then it's just a matter of getting them out of the pan to serve!

ALMOND & ORANGE BISCOTTI

MAKES **12**

PREP **15** mins, plus cooling

COOK **50** mins

¾ cup all-purpose flour, plus extra for dusting

1 teaspoon baking powder

pinch of salt

2 tablespoons butter, softened

⅓ cup granulated sugar

1 egg

⅓ cup chopped almonds

1 teaspoons freshly squeezed orange juice

grated rind of ½ orange

1 teaspoon orange liqueur

2 ounces semisweet, milk, or white chocolate, broken into pieces, to decorate (optional)

1 Preheat the oven to 350°F. Mix together the flour, baking powder, and salt in a medium bowl.

2 Cream the butter and sugar together with a wooden spoon or an electric mixer until light and fluffy. Add the egg and beat until combined. Stir in the almonds, orange juice and rind, and liqueur. Gradually add the flour mixture and mix until well combined.

3 Line a baking sheet with nonstick parchment paper and dust it lightly with flour. Turn out the dough on the sheet and shape it into a 3¼ × 8-inch flattened log.

4 Bake the log for 30 minutes or until the dough is golden and firm to the touch. Let cool for at least 15 minutes. Cut the log at an angle into twelve ½-inch slices. Place these on the baking sheet and bake for 8 minutes, then turn and bake for 8 minutes until golden. Cool on a wire rack.

5 If using, melt the chocolate in a heatproof bowl set over a saucepan of barely simmering water, making sure the bottom of the bowl doesn't touch the water below. Let cool a little, then transfer to a pastry bag. Decorate the biscotti by piping the chocolate over them.

Two delicacies dancing together on a sea of lace ... One will take you moments to prepare; the other will require patience and practice. Both are bites of melodious heaven and will have your young ladies pirouetting to the table again and again.

COCONUT SQUARES

MAKES **24**

PREP **10** mins, plus chilling

1 (14-ounce) can condensed milk

4 cups confectioners' sugar, sifted

4 cups shredded dried coconut

few drops of pink or red food coloring

1 Line an 8-inch square, loose-bottom cake pan with nonstick parchment paper.

2 Mix together the milk and confectioners' sugar in a large bowl. Add the dried coconut gradually until the mixture is firm but not crumbling apart. To test, take a walnut-size ball of the mixture and press it in the palm of your hand. If it holds its shape, it's ready, but if it sags or is very sticky, add more coconut.

3 Press half the mixture into the prepared cake pan. Mix a few drops of food coloring into the remaining half of the mixture and work the color through thoroughly, then press the colored mixture on top of the white layer in the cake pan. Chill the mixture in the refrigerator for 2 hours to let it harden.

4 Cut into 24 squares to serve.

CHOCOLATE MACAROONS WITH PEARLS

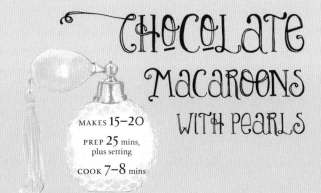

MAKES **15–20**

PREP **25** mins, plus setting

COOK **7–8** mins

For the macaroons

¾ cup ground almonds

1¼ cups confectioners' sugar

3 tablespoons unsweetened cocoa powder

2 egg whites, beaten until stiff peaks form

For the filling

⅓ cup heavy whipping cream

⅓ cup mascarpone cheese

¼ cup confectioners' sugar

seeds from 1 vanilla beans

¼ cup edible sugar pearls or beads (available online)

1 Preheat the oven to 350°F. Line a baking sheet with nonstick parchment paper.

2 For the macaroons, mix the almonds, sugar, and cocoa powder in a bowl. Fold in the egg whites. Transfer to a pastry bag. Pipe fifteen to twenty 1¼-inch circles onto the baking sheet. Let set for 15 minutes. Bake for 7–8 minutes with the oven door slightly ajar.

3 To remove the macaroons from the paper, lift one corner of the paper and pour some boiled water onto the baking sheet. As water hits the underside of the paper, the macaroons lift off easily without sticking.

4 To make the filling, beat together the cream, mascarpone, sugar, and vanilla seeds in a bowl. Spoon the mixture into a pastry bag fitted with a ½-inch plain tip. Line up the macaroons in two lines. Pipe a generous dollop of cream onto half of them, then top each with an uncovered one and press gently.

5 Place the edible pearls on a large plate and gently roll the filled macaroons through them to cover the sides with the pearls.

At every party there must be a dish that whisks you off on a fairy-tale journey to a place where only you and the dessert will live happily ever after. These mini tarts capture this moment perfectly. Pear and chocolate are natural bedfellows, and the mint adds a fantastic burst of freshness.

PeaR & MiNt CHoColate MiNi TaRts

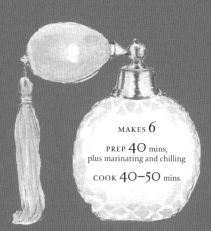

MAKES 6

PREP 40 mins, plus marinating and chilling

COOK 40–50 mins

1 vanilla bean

1 bottle of red wine

1 cup superfine sugar or granulated sugar

1 cinnamon stick, snapped in half

few sprigs of mint

4 pears, peeled but kept whole

For the chocolate ganache

4 ounces semisweet chocolate, broken into pieces

½ cup heavy cream

1 ounce mint (about ⅓ bunch)

1 tablespoon butter

For the pastry dough

⅓ cup confectioners sugar

⅓ cup unsweetened cocoa powder

¾ cup all-purpose flour, plus extra for dusting

4 tablespoons butter, chilled

1 egg yolk

1 Halve the vanilla bean lengthwise, scrape out the black seeds, and put them in a large saucepan with the wine, sugar, cinnamon, and mint. Cut each piece of bean into three long, thin strips and add them to pan, then lower the pears into the pan.

2 Poach the pears, covered, for about 20–30 minutes, depending on their ripeness—once cooked, they should be tender all the way through when pierced with a toothpick. (Try not to overcook them, because this will make slicing them difficult later on.) Let the pears cool in the wine and let them marinate for at least 3 hours, or overnight, to soak up the color.

3 For the ganache, put the chocolate in a heatproof bowl. Heat the cream and mint in a small saucepan until bubbles form at the edges. Strain the cream, pouring it onto the chocolate. Stir until the chocolate melts and combines with the cream, then add the butter and stir again. Let the mixture cool, then chill in the refrigerator for 30–60 minutes.

4 To make the pastry dough, mix the confectioners' sugar, cocoa powder, and flour in a large bowl. Cut the butter into small cubes and rub it into the dry ingredients with your fingertips until the mixture resembles bread crumbs. Add the egg yolk and combine. The dough should form a ball, but if it is still dry and crumbly, slowly add up to 1 tablespoon iced water, making sure the dough does not get too wet. Wrap the dough with plastic wrap and chill in the refrigerator for about 30 minutes.

5 Preheat the oven to 325°F. Roll out the dough on a lightly floured work surface to ⅛ inch thick and cut out six 5½-inch-diameter circles. Press them into six 3½-inch diameter cups in a muffin pan. Trim any overlapping dough to neaten. Cut out circles of nonstick parchment paper, place them on the dough, then fill with pie weights or dried beans. Bake for 10 minutes. Remove the paper and weights and bake for a few more minutes until the pastry has hardened, then let cool.

6 Unmold and fill the pastry shells with the ganache. (If it is still soft, refrigerate the tarts for an hour or so until firm.) Slice the pears in half lengthwise, then cut into thin slices. Arrange on top of each tart in a rose shape—use the photograph as a guide.

No party for a young lady is complete without the all-important mocktail! The two recipes given here are my personal favorites, but I insist you tailor them to your own taste. The excitement is in the making and experimenting. I had a pink cocktail maker in my teenage years, and I loved mixing fruits, balancing flavors, and making things fizz. So cheers, my beautiful young dears! May your teenage years be full of happiness.

MOCKTAILS

VIRGIN STRAWBERRY DAIQUIRI

SERVES 6
PREP 2 mins

¾ cup frozen strawberries
pinch of salt
1 teaspoon sugar
4 ice cubes

1 Place the strawberries, salt, sugar, and ice cubes in a blender and blend the concoction until smooth. Serve chilled, in grown-up cocktail glasses.

VIRGIN APPLE FIZZ

SERVES 6
PREP 2 mins

½ cup apple juice
½ teaspoon lemon juice
1 teaspoon sugar syrup
crushed ice
sparkling water

1 Put the juices and sugar syrup in a cocktail shaker with crushed ice and shake for 5–10 seconds. Strain the mixture into six glasses, then fill the rest of each glass with sparkling water.

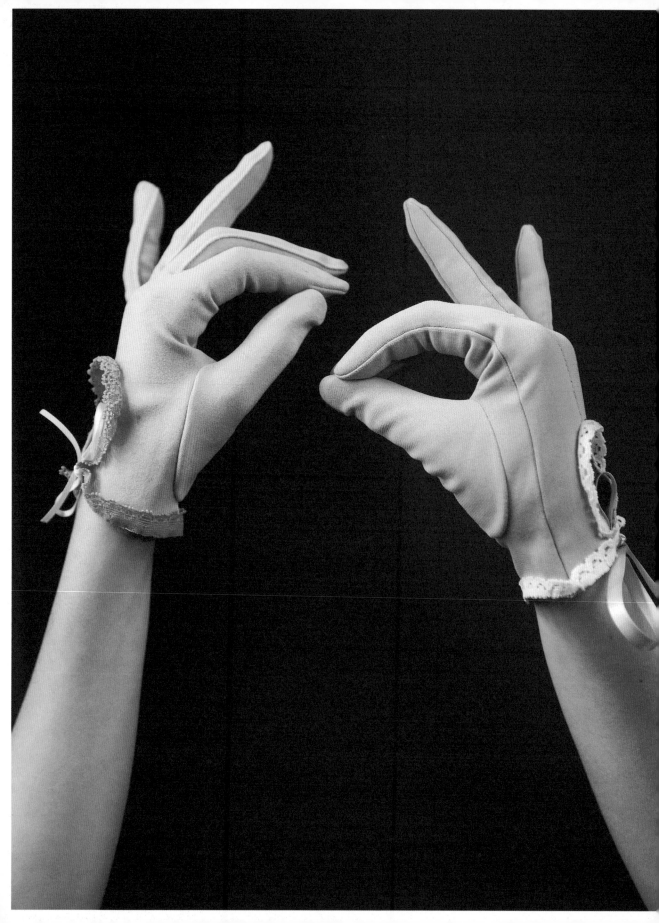

How to Make Elegant Cutout Gloves

What should a chic young woman wear to her coming-of-age party? Elegant gloves, of course! You can show these off as you daintily eat and drink the splendid delicacies being offered. And the best part? When asked where you got them from, you can mention how you customized them, so they are the only pair like this in the whole world!

YOU WILL NEED

✄ pair of fabric gloves (not knitted, suede, or leather) ✄ thin marker pen ✄ fabric scissors ✄ 1 yard pretty elastic lace ✄ needle and thread to match the color of your gloves ✄ ½ yard thin ribbon in a shade that complements the color of your gloves

1 Put on one glove and, using your other hand and a thin marker pen, draw a teardrop shape on the back of your hand where you would like the cutout section to be. Start off small—you can always make it larger if you want to. When you are happy with the shape, cut it out, and use it as a template to cut out exactly the same shape on the second glove.

2 Now attach the elastic lace to the cuff and cutout section of each glove. Begin at a side seam, with the bottom edge of the elastic in line with the cuff. Use a small blanket stitch to join the two together, easing the elastic around the curve of the cutout section. Try

to just bend instead of pulling the elastic tight; pulling can result in a misshapen glove.

3 When you have sewn the elastic on all the way around the bottom of the glove, cut off any remaining elastic. Use a couple of stitches to join the ends of the elastic neatly.

4 Cut two pieces of ribbon, each 4 inches long, and sew one to the wrong side of the glove fabric at each side of the bottom of your teardrop shape, at the cuff. When finished, tie the ribbon into a pretty bow.

5 Repeat this process on the other glove to complete the pair.

HOW TO CREATE THE
Hair Bow

It was only in the 1950s that the word "teenager" was created; before then, young ladies were expected to be little adults in training and were taught the finer details of how to take care of a household. Playing grown-ups can certainly be fun, and this hairdo is sophisticated, yet very clearly shouts "I'm still a teenager!"

YOU WILL NEED

hairband bristle brush hairspray section clips and hairpins tail comb

◁ **STEP 1** Gather your hair into a ponytail at the top of the head and secure it with a hairband, making sure that any flyaway strands are smoothed and sprayed into place. (If the ponytail is not sitting on the top of the head, the "bow" will not be upright.)

◁ **STEP 3** Take one of the two outer sections of hair and tease along its entire length. Spray this teased section of hair liberally with hairspray and smooth the hair gently with a bristle brush.

▷ **STEP 2** Divide the ponytail into three even sections. Use a section clip to hold each section of the ponytail separately.

▷ **STEP 4** Pull the teased section horizontally and fold the hair in half. Bring the ends of this section to the bottom of the ponytail, creating one half of the bow. Secure it with hairpins. Repeat steps 3 and 4 with the other outer section of the ponytail, creating the other half of the bow. Leave the middle section clipped out of the way.

◁ **STEP 5** Take the middle
section of hair and wrap
it over the front of the
ponytail to cover the
hairband, then divide the hair
to wind each section underneath
each side of the bow. How many
times you wrap the hair around the bow
will depend on the length of the hair, but try to
create a neat vertical fold of hair, which produces
the bow effect.

▷ **STEP 6** Use hairpins
to secure the bottom
of the bow.

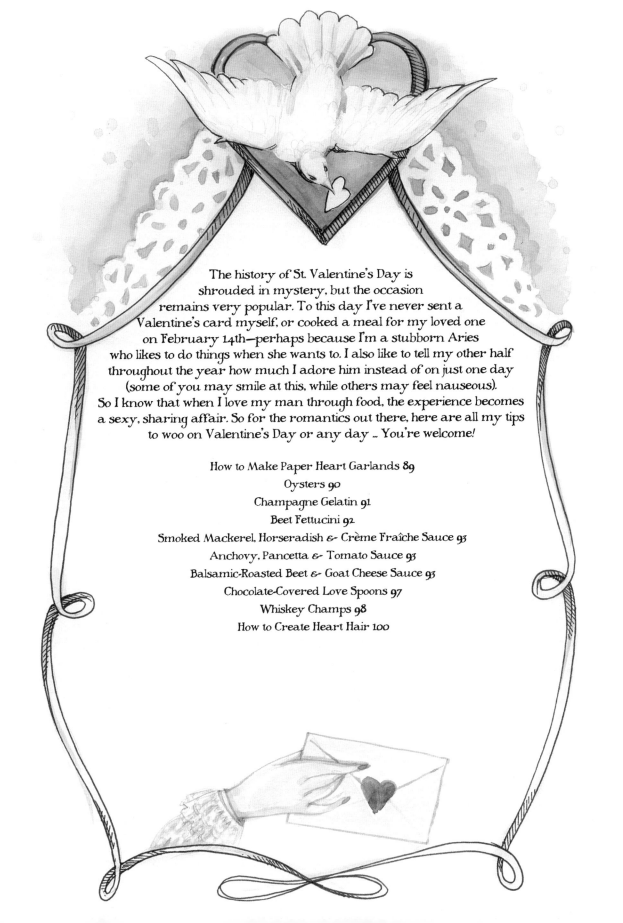

The history of St. Valentine's Day is shrouded in mystery, but the occasion remains very popular. To this day I've never sent a Valentine's card myself, or cooked a meal for my loved one on February 14th—perhaps because I'm a stubborn Aries who likes to do things when she wants to. I also like to tell my other half throughout the year how much I adore him instead of on just one day (some of you may smile at this, while others may feel nauseous). So I know that when I love my man through food, the experience becomes a sexy, sharing affair. So for the romantics out there, here are all my tips to woo on Valentine's Day or any day ... You're welcome!

HOW TO MAKE PAPER HEART GARLANDS

Giving your heart away has never been so much fun! Collect maps, receipts, postcards, and any other scraps of paper from places you and your Valentine have visited to give your paper heart sentiment and meaning. One heart is all you need, but why stop there? Show off! Hang garlands from the ceiling and around the table, and welcome your partner into the love cave! Cheesy? Hell, yeah!

YOU WILL NEED

♡ maps, receipts, postcards, or other paper to make the hearts ♡ paper scissors

♡ stapler ♡ ribbon—cut the length you want your garlands to hang

1 First, you need to make the paper strips that form your hearts. You'll need three different sizes of strip—we used strips measuring 1¼ × 4½ inches, 1¼ × 6½ inches, and 1¼ × 8½ inches. You need two of each size to form one heart, so cut enough for the number of hearts you want to make.

2 Take one strip of each size and lay these on top of each other so that they are lined up along one of the 1¼-inch edges. Hold them together along the bottom and, one by one, bend the other 1¼-inch edges over to line up with the aligned edges. All the 1¼-inch edges should now be held

together, creating half a heart shape. Staple this shape at the aligned edges to secure it. Now repeat the step to make the second half of a heart shape.

3 Find the point on your ribbon where you want your hearts to start. Line up your two heart halves on each side of the ribbon so that the ribbon runs between them, then staple the paper in place.

4 Repeat the previous steps as many times as you like, filling your hanging garland with hearts. Or make just a single heart to hang as a decoration.

OYSTERS

¾ cup raspberries

¼ cup red wine vinegar

1 shallot, finely chopped

1 teaspoon black pepper

pinch of flaked sea salt

12 chilled fresh oysters

crushed ice

kosher salt, to serve

1 Press the raspberries through a strainer with a wooden spoon or a rubber spatula to remove the seeds. Discard the seeds.

2 In a small bowl, combine the raspberry puree with the red wine vinegar, shallot, and black pepper. Season with the salt.

3 Shuck and loosen the oysters from their shells, but leave them in their shells for ease of eating. Store the oysters on crushed ice.

4 Spoon about 1 teaspoon of the raspberry vinegar onto each oyster and serve on a bed of kosher salt.

The beauty of gelatin is in the gentle wobble of the set. Any vessel can showcase this refreshing palate cleanser. I love the classic combination of strawberries with Champagne, but use any berry you want and be creative with what you serve it in.

CHAMPAGNE GELATIN

SERVES **2**
PREP **15** mins, plus chilling
COOK **5** mins

1 tablespoon plain powdered gelatin
1 cup Champagne
2 strawberries, sliced

1 Place the gelatin in a saucepan and pour the Champagne over it. Let stand for 5 minutes, then place the mixture over low heat and slowly let the gelatin dissolve, occasionally stirring gently with a spatula. Do not let the mixture boil. Once the gelatin has dissolved, take the pan off the heat and let cool a little.

2 Divide the Champagne between 2 small heart-shape ramekins or pretty dishes. Tap the dishes firmly on the work surface to release any air bubbles. Place a few strawberry slices in each dish. Refrigerate for 1–1½ hours, until firm.

Food made with love tastes better—fact. Give yourself time to prepare this dish, especially if this is your first time making pasta, and try getting the best-quality pasta flour, if you can. With the hard work done and your amazing, earthy pasta in the saucepan, show off a little more by creating three simple but delicious pasta sauces. Your other half will be spinning with excitement and won't know where to put his fork first!

SERVES 2

PREP 30 mins, plus resting

COOK 10 mins

Beet Fettucini

2½ cups "00" flour, pasta flour, or all-purpose plus extra for dusting

2 free-range eggs and 1 free-range egg yolk

salt

½ cup cooked beet, pureed

1 Place the flour in a mound in the center of a large work surface and make a well in the middle. Pour the eggs and egg yolk into the well and add a pinch of salt and 2 large tablespoons of the pureed beet.

2 Using a fork, beat the egg mixture, slowly incorporating the flour, beginning at the inner rim of the well. When the flour is incorporated, gather the dough together to form a rounded mass. Begin kneading the dough with the palms of your hands. If it seems too stiff, add a little more of the pureed beet. If it seems too sticky, add more flour.

3 Knead the dough on a lightly floured work surface for 5–10 minutes, until it is smooth and elastic. Wrap the dough in plastic wrap, place it in a bowl, and let it rest for 30 minutes at room temperature.

4 Divide the dough into eight equal pieces and pat them flat. Lightly flour the pieces and cover them with plastic wrap until you are ready to press them. Pass the first piece through the widest setting of your pasta machine twice, each time folding it in half before rolling it through again. Continue rolling the dough in this way, setting the machine one step smaller and passing the dough through twice on each setting.

5 Attach the pasta cutter to the machine and run the lengths of dough through it. Lightly coat the fettucini with flour and let it rest, or hang it up in strips for about 10 minutes to dry.

6 Bring a large saucepan of salted water to a boil. Add the remaining beet to the pasta water. Add the pasta and cook for 3 minutes. Drain and serve one-third of the pasta with each of the individual sauces.

SMOKED MACKEREL,
HORSERADISH & CRÈME FRAÎCHE SAUCE

PREP 5 mins

COOK 10 mins

1 tablespoon olive oil

1 shallot, chopped

⅓ cup white wine

½ cup crème fraîche or sour cream

1 tablespoon horseradish sauce

grated rind and juice of ½ lemon

4 ounces smoked mackerel, flaked

salt and black pepper

chopped dill, to garnish

1 Heat the oil in a skillet set over medium heat. Add the shallot and sauté until softened.

2 Add the white wine. Bring the mixture to a boil and simmer for about 5 minutes, until the liquid volume is reduced by half.

3 Add the crème fraîche or sour cream, horseradish sauce, lemon rind and juice, flaked mackerel, and seasoning and stir well to combine.

4 Let the sauce warm through, then take it off the heat, add the cooked pasta, and toss together. Serve immediately, garnished with dill.

ANCHOVY, PANCETTA
& TOMATO SAUCE

PREP 5 mins

COOK 15 mins

2 ounces pancetta, finely diced

½ shallot, finely diced

½ cup red wine

1 tomato, chopped

1 tablespoon chopped parsley

4 anchovy fillets in oil, drained and coarsely chopped

½ tablespoon chopped capers

1 Dry-fry the pancetta over gentle heat.

2 Add the shallot and cook it in the fat released from the pancetta until it has softened.

3 Add the wine, chopped tomatoes, parsley, anchovy fillets, and capers, then simmer the sauce for 10 minutes.

4 Take the sauce off the heat, add the cooked pasta, and toss together. Serve immediately.

BALSAMIC-ROASTED BEET
& GOAT CHEESE SAUCE

PREP 5 mins

COOK 1 hour

2 beets, peeled and quartered

2 tablespoons olive oil

1 tablespoon balsamic vinegar

1 small red onion, finely chopped

leaves from 2 sprigs of thyme

½ cup crème fraîche or sour cream

2 ounces goat cheese, chopped into small pieces

Parmesan cheese, to serve

1 Preheat the oven to 400°F. Toss the beets in half the oil and vinegar, place in a roasting pan, and roast for 45 minutes, until cooked through.

2 Meanwhile, heat the remaining oil and vinegar in a saucepan and sauté the onion until softened. Add the thyme leaves. Transfer the beets to the pan, then add the crème fraîche or sour cream. Simmer over low heat until the crème fraîche is runny and the sauce is pink. Add the goat cheese.

3 Remove the sauce from the heat, add the cooked pasta, and toss together. Serve immediately with some grated Parmesan.

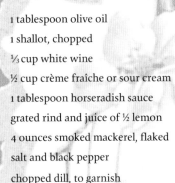

smoked Mackerel
Pasta sauce

Beet & Goat
Cheese Pasta sauce

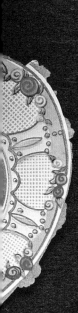

It's been proven that eating chocolate triggers the release of the happy hormone serotonin, promoting feelings of pleasure. So this chapter on love simply would not be complete without a lick of this good stuff. These love spoons are the grown-up version of a lollipop, and each time I make them I vary the flavors slightly to keep them interesting. So my man never knows exactly what he's putting in his mouth!

CHOCOLATE-COVERED love SPOONS

MAKES **4**

PREP **15** mins, plus chilling

COOK **5** mins

3 ounces semisweet chocolate

1 tablespoon brandy

pinch of chili powder

¼ teaspoon ground cinnamon

pinch of ground nutmeg

1 Break the chocolate into pieces and melt it in a heatproof bowl set over a saucepan of barely simmering water, making sure the bottom of the bowl doesn't touch the water below. Reserve 3 tablespoons of melted chocolate in another bowl for coating.

2 In a bowl, combine the brandy and spices with the melted chocolate. Fill the bowls of four ornate spoons with the melted-chocolate mixture, then set them on a tray and place them in the refrigerator for 10 minutes to let the chocolate harden a little.

3 Remove the spoons from the refrigerator and coat them with the remaining melted chocolate. Let chill once again until hard.

4 Serve the spoons with hot after-dinner drinks.

I may have mentioned before that my favorite drink is Champagne. But as a giving and sharing girlfriend, I don't like to be too selfish, so I've incorporated my man's favorite drink, whiskey, in this recipe. The two are a match made in heaven!

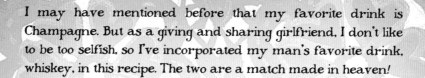

WHISKEY CHAMPS

SERVES **2**

PREP **5** mins

¼ cup whiskey

1 tablespoon framboise

1 cup Champagne or sparkling wine

1 If you're planning to serve this cocktail in a "love cup," as we have done, simply pour the whiskey and framboise into the cup and top up with bubbly, then share with your loved one. Alternatively, divide the whiskey and the crème de frambois between two Champagne flutes, then fill to the top of the flutes with bubbly.

How to Create
HEART HAIR

Why stop at food to show your love? With this cheeky hairdo, you can wear your heart just a bit north of your sleeve, and remind your man that you love him with every part of you—mind, body, soul ... and hair!

YOU WILL NEED

✎ hair mousse ✎ tail comb ✎ curling tongs ✎ bobby pins, curl clips (optional), and hairpins ✎ section clips ✎ hairspray ✎ bristle brush

HOW TO CURL AND SET

The first step with most vintage hairstyles is to curl and set the hair.

To do this, apply some mousse liberally through the length of your hair and comb it through.

Taking sections of less than ½ inch, curl the hair horizontally, using your curling tongs and secure into pin curls with bobby pins or curl clips.

If you don't have the time to sleep in your set and have decided to style it on the day, just let your hair cool for about 15–20 minutes.

▽ **STEP 1** After you have curled and set your hair (*see box, left*), part your hair, using a tail comb, into your desired parting. A centered parting is recommended for symmetry with the heart-shape victory rolls. Divide the hair into four sections by parting it from front to back and across the top of the head, from ear to ear. Secure the sections with section clips.

▷ **STEP 2** Position bobby pins in a vertical line about 2 inches away from the centered parting on each side. Making sure the pins overlap slightly provides a tighter, more secure hairstyle.

◁ **STEP 3** Lightly tease one of the back sections of hair with your tail comb and spray with hairspray. Taking a bristle brush, smooth this section of hair gently from the nape of the neck upward.

▷ **STEP 4** Roll one back section while pinching the ends of the hair under the roll, sweeping the roll toward the parting. Once you have your desired shape, use hairpins to hold it in place.

◁ **STEP 5** Repeat step 4 on the other back section of hair. Make sure these two back victory rolls are a similar size to produce a symmetrical heart shape.

◁ **STEP 6** Now work on one of the front sections of hair. Tease and smooth it gently with a bristle brush. Form a victory roll at the front, making sure it is in line with the back roll, and secure it with hairpins. Repeat this step with the other front section of hair. Next, carefully connect the top of one of the back rolls and the back of its corresponding front victory roll, using hairpins to make the join seamless. Repeat on the other side. Spray liberally with hairspray, using the palm of your hand to smooth over any stray hairs.

BACHELORETTE PARTY

Angel: "Hello, welcome to The Vintage Patisserie."

Customer: "Hello, I would like to enquire about a stylish bachelorette party that my friends will love as well as my mom and my gran!"

Angel: "Fabulous, my dear, you have come to exactly the right place."

A staggering 75 percent of our tea parties are for fervent brides-to-be, all of them with the same objectives in mind: fun, laughter, naughtiness, and elegance. I'm pretty sure I've got this covered for you, so all you need to think about is how to tackle your hangover!

My continued obsession with anything edibly "rose" was the inspiration for this dish. The spicy meatball-like kofta bites kick off a party in your mouth, while the refreshing and aromatic rose gelatin lifts and refreshes your palate—allowing you to have that extra kofta and head right back to the party!

Lamb Kofta with Rose Gelatin

SERVES 12

PREP 15 mins, plus cooling/chilling

COOK 15 mins

For the rose gelatin

1 cup granulated sugar

1¾ tablespoons plain powdered gelatin

2 tablespoons rosewater

1 tablespoon edible dried rose petals (available online)

1 Heat the sugar with 2 cups water in a saucepan over medium heat until the sugar has melted. Let the syrup cool, then add the gelatin and rosewater and let sit for 5 minutes. Heat the pan gently until the gelatin dissolves—do not let it boil. Remove the gelatin from the heat and pour it into 12 shot glasses, sprinkle with the rose petals, and let stand in the refrigerator to set.

For the kofta meatballs

8 ounces ground lamb

¼ small onion, chopped

¾ cup fresh white bread crumbs

¼ cup chopped parsley

2 tablespoons chopped mint

1 garlic clove, finely chopped

¼ teaspoon ground cumin

¼ teaspoon ground cinnamon

¼ teaspoon ground ginger

¼ teaspoon salt

pinch of black pepper

2 teaspoons harissa

1 extra-large egg

sunflower oil, for pan-frying

1 Mix together all the ingredients except the oil in a large bowl with your hands. Shape the mixture into 24 small balls, set them on a plate, cover with plastic wrap, and chill in the refrigerator for 30 minutes.

2 Heat a little oil in a skillet over medium heat. Cook the kofta meatballs for about 5 minutes, until golden and cooked through, then drain on paper towels. Skewer them with toothpicks and place one on top of each rose gelatin shot glass. Place the extra kofta meatballs on a plate, for seconds.

When you are organizing a bachelorette party for a close friend, there have to be one or two dishes that satisfy the soul and are simple to prepare. I think of this favorite as a gourmet pizza: crisp, juicy, and full of flavor! In fact, don't be tied down to this recipe—your only limitation is what's in the refrigerator!

RATATOUILLE TART

SERVES 6

PREP 20 mins

COOK
25–30 mins

1 zucchini

1 eggplant

1 red bell pepper

1 sheet ready-to-bake all-butter
puff pastry, thawed if frozen

all-purpose flour, for dusting

3 tablespoons tomato puree

2 tablespoons extra-virgin olive oil

salt and black pepper

1 egg, beaten, or milk, to glaze

leaves from 2 sprigs of basil

1 tablespoon grated Parmesan cheese (optional)

1 Preheat the oven to 350°F.

2 Line a large baking sheet with nonstick parchment paper. Slice the zucchini, eggplant, and bell pepper into $^1/_{16}$-inch-thick circles.

3 Roll out the pastry dough on a lightly floured work surface to a 7 × 12-inch rectangle, neatening the edges with a long sharp knife. Lightly score a ¾-inch border around the edges of the dough and gently pierce inside the border with a fork.

4 Spread the dough with the tomato puree, then layer the vegetables in alternating rows on top. Drizzle 1 tablespoon of the olive oil over the vegetables and season. Brush the edges of the pastry with the egg or milk.

5 Bake the tart for 25–30 minutes or until the vegetables are softened and the pastry is cooked through, risen, and golden. Remove from the oven; sprinkle with the basil, the 1 tablespoon olive oil, and Parmesan, if using.

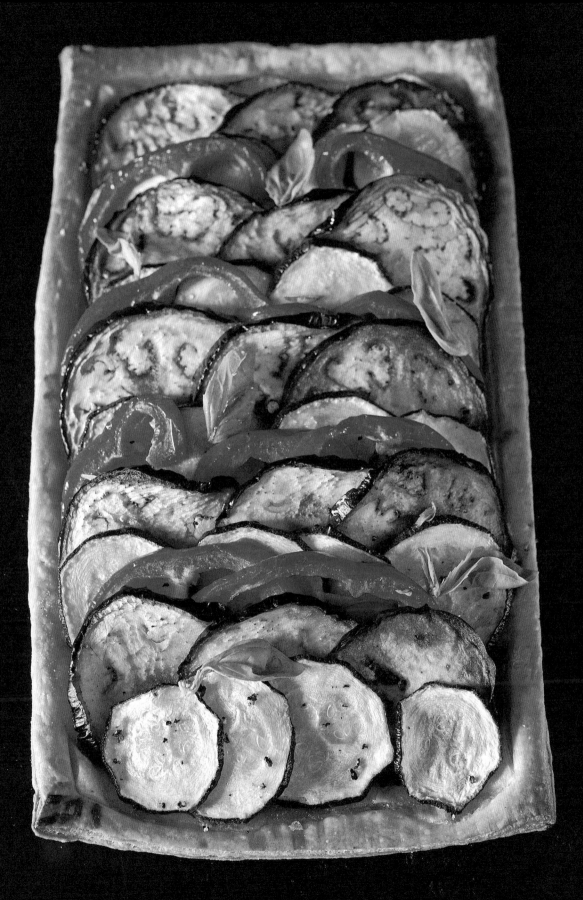

When you're giggling and chattering away with your wonderful girlfriends, what could be better than popping a perfectly formed bite-size piece of tastiness into your mouth? These filling little delights really do explode in the mouth and hit the spot and, what's better, is that they give you one hand free to ... well, drink! For your vegetarian girlfriends, swap the pork for their favorite cheese-and-onion mixture.

Rice Balls

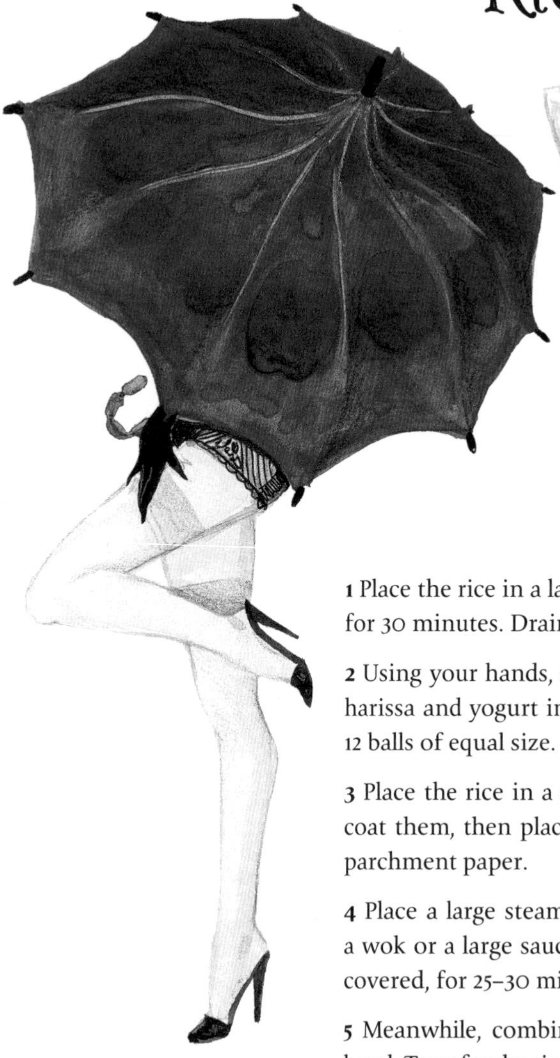

SERVES **6**
PREP **15** mins, plus soaking
COOK **25–30** mins

1 cup long-grain rice

1 pound ground pork

1 tablespoon all-purpose flour

2 teaspoons ras el hanout

½ onion, diced

½ small carrot, peeled and grated

2 tablespoons slivered almonds

⅓ cup dried chopped apricots

2 tablespoons chopped cilantro

1 teaspoon–1 tablespoon harissa

½ cup plain yogurt

1 Place the rice in a large bowl, cover it with cold water, and let soak for 30 minutes. Drain the rice well.

2 Using your hands, combine the remaining ingredients except the harissa and yogurt in a separate bowl, then shape the mixture into 12 balls of equal size.

3 Place the rice in a shallow dish. Roll the lamb balls in the rice to coat them, then place them on a baking sheet lined with nonstick parchment paper.

4 Place a large steamer lined with nonstick parchment paper over a wok or a large saucepan of simmering water. Cook the rice balls, covered, for 25–30 minutes or until cooked through.

5 Meanwhile, combine the harissa (to taste) and yogurt in a small bowl. Transfer the rice balls to a plate and serve with the harissa sauce.

Originally from the Philippines, the sweet potato has become quite a favorite of us Brits. Personally, I like to "crisp, salt, and eat" these flavorful bites, and they are the perfect accompaniment for everything! However, be careful—they can make you a little thirsty, so you might have to drink another cocktail to quench your thirst. Oh, it's a hard life!

SWEET POTATO CHIPS

SERVES 8

PREP 15 mins

COOK 15 mins

2 teaspoons sea salt flakes

½ teaspoon black pepper

½ teaspoon sweet paprika

½ teaspoon finely grated lemon rind

2 medium sweet potatoes, peeled

vegetable oil, for deep-frying

1 Combine the salt, black pepper, paprika, and lemon rind in a skillet over low heat. Cook, stirring, for 1 minute or until fragrant. Remove the mixture from the heat and set it aside.

2 Use a vegetable peeler to cut the sweet potatoes into long, thin ribbons. Place these on a baking sheet lined with paper towels.

3 Heat 4 inches oil over medium-high heat to 350°F. (When the oil is hot enough, a cube of bread dropped into it will turn golden brown in 15 seconds.)

4 Deep-fry handfuls of the chips for 30 seconds or until golden, stirring gently with a slotted spoon so that they don't stick to the pan. Transfer the cooked chips to the prepared baking sheet, and season with the salt mixture. Repeat the process with the remaining sweet potato and salt mixture. Serve immediately, or store the chips in an airtight container for a few days.

These little bites earn their ranking as one of the sweetest, smokiest, saltiest, and most scrumptious party snacks in this book purely on its British name alone! There is a similar version that's made using oysters, called "Angels on Horseback" and, yes, that's exactly how I plan to be transported home when my Prince Charming comes to pick me up at the end of my hen do!

DaTe DeVILS ON HORSebaCK

MAKES **24**

PREP **20** mins

COOK **10–15** mins

1 cup smoked almonds

4 tablespoons butter,
at room temperature

24 pitted Medjool dates

6 thin slices of rindless bacon

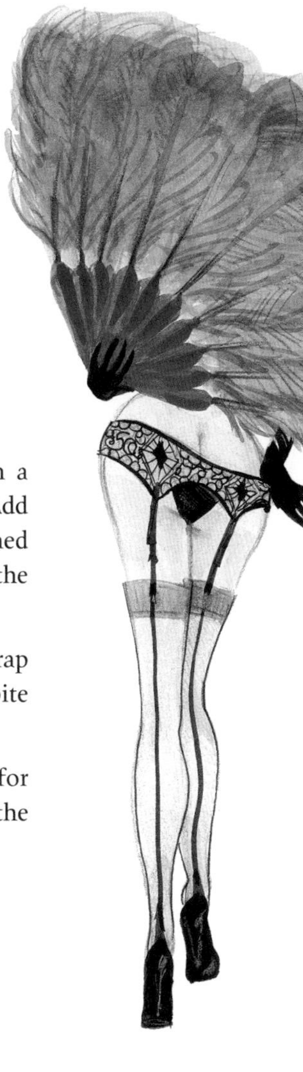

1 Preheat the oven to 350°F. Process the almonds in a food processor until they are coarsely chopped. Add the butter and process again until it is well combined with the almonds. Divide the mixture evenly among the date cavities.

2 Cut each slice of bacon crosswise into four pieces. Wrap a piece of bacon around each date. Skewer each bite with a toothpick.

3 Place the bites on a baking sheet and bake them for about 10–15 minutes or until the bacon is cooked and the stuffing is heated through.

A mischievous ladies' gathering is incomplete without sweetness of the edible kind. These three cherry-picked delights will complement the night with a kiss. Pop a Maraschino Cookie to fuel some dance moves, or a Raspberry Custard Tart for a sweet-sharp taste sensation, or lose yourself in a Red Velvet Layer Cake. I challenge anyone not to feel seduced after these.

Raspberry Custard Tarts

MAKES 24

PREP 30 mins, plus chilling and infusing

COOK 25 mins

1 store-bought rolled dough pie crust, thawed if frozen

24 raspberries

confectioners' sugar, for dusting (optional)

For the crème patissière

1 vanilla bean, split lengthwise

½ cup milk

1 egg yolk

1 tablespoon all-purpose flour, plus extra for dusting

2 tablespoons superfine sugar

2 tablespoons heavy whipping cream

1 To make the tarts, on a work surface dusted with flour, roll out the dough to a thickness of about ½ inch. Using a pastry cutter, stamp out 24 circles, just larger than the cups of a mini-muffin pan (you may need to reroll the trimmings to have enough dough). Gently press a dough circle into each of the cups of two 12-cup mini-muffin pans. Prick the bottom of each pastry shell with a fork, then line them with parchment paper and fill with pie weights or dried beans. Place the muffin pans in the refrigerator to chill for 20 minutes. Preheat the oven to 375°F.

2 Bake the tart shells for 10 minutes, then carefully remove the paper and weights and bake for another 3–5 minutes, until the pastry has set and is pale golden. Let cool.

3 To make the crème patissière, use a small sharp knife to scrape the seeds from the vanilla bean. Cook the vanilla bean, seeds, and milk in a small saucepan set over medium heat, stirring, for 5 minutes or until the mixture just comes to a simmer. Take the pan off the heat, cover with the lid, and set aside for 20 minutes to steep, then remove the vanilla bean.

4 Combine the egg yolk, flour, and sugar in a bowl and beat with a handheld electric mixer until thick and pale. Next, beat in the steeped milk. Heat the mixture in a clean saucepan set over medium heat. Cook, stirring continuously, for 4–5 minutes or until the mixture boils and thickens, then strain it through a fine strainer into a bowl and cover the surface with plastic wrap to prevent a skin from forming. Chill in the refrigerator for 40 minutes.

5 Remove the chilled cream from the refrigerator and beat it until smooth. Add the heavy whipping cream and continue to beat until well combined. Spoon the crème patissière evenly among the pastry shells. Top each tart with a raspberry and dust with confectioners' sugar, if desired. Serve immediately.

MARASCHINO COOKIES

MAKES **18**

PREP **20** mins, plus chilling

COOK **15** mins

1 stick butter, softened

½ cup granulated sugar

¼ cup firmly packed dark brown sugar

¼ teaspoon salt

1 egg

1 teaspoon vanilla extract

1¼ cups all-purpose flour

⅔ cup unsweetened cocoa powder

¼ teaspoon baking soda

¼ teaspoon baking powder

18 maraschino or candied cherries

1 Preheat the oven to 400°F. Line two baking sheets with nonstick parchment paper.

2 Cream the butter and sugars together with a wooden spoon or an electric mixer until light and fluffy. Add the salt, egg, and vanilla extract and beat well.

3 In a separate bowl, combine the flour, cocoa powder, baking soda, and baking powder. Slowly fold the dry ingredients into the creamed butter mixture until a smooth dough forms. It should be solid enough to hold its shape when rolled into a ball. Wrap the dough in plastic wrap and chill in the refrigerator for 30 minutes.

4 Remove the dough from the refrigerator, unwrap it, and roll it into 18 balls that are about 1¼ inches in diameter. Place these on the prepared baking sheet. Using your thumb, make a small cherry-size indentation in the top of each ball of dough. Place a cherry in each of these indentations.

5 Bake the cookies for 15 minutes. Take them out of the oven and let them cool for about 5 minutes, then transfer the cookies to a wire rack to cool completely.

RED VELVET LAYER CAKE

4 tablespoons unsalted butter, softened, plus extra for greasing

⅔ cup granulated sugar

1 egg, beaten

1 teaspoon vanilla extract

⅔ cup all-purpose flour, plus extra for dusting

1½ tablespoons unsweetened cocoa powder

1 teaspoon baking soda

pinch of salt

2 teaspoons red food coloring

¼ cup buttermilk

For the frosting

4 tablespoons unsalted butter, softened

½ cup cream cheese

1⅔ cups confectioners' sugar

½ teaspoon vanilla extract

½ cup chopped pecans

MAKES **6**

PREP **15** mins

COOK **30** mins

1 Preheat the oven to 350°F. Grease and flour an 8-inch square, loose-bottom cake pan. Cream the butter and sugar together with a wooden spoon or an electric mixer until light and fluffy. Beat in the egg and vanilla extract. Sift the flour, cocoa, baking soda, and salt into a separate bowl. Stir the food coloring into the buttermilk, then mix this and the flour mixture alternately into the creamed mixture. Pour the batter into the pan and bake for 25–30 minutes, until firm. Let the cake cool in the pan for 10 minutes, then turn it out on a wire rack and let it cool completely.

2 For the frosting, beat the butter and cream cheese together in a bowl. Beat in the sugar and vanilla extract.

3 Halve the sponge into two 4-inch-wide pieces. Cut each half into five 1½-inch-wide rectangles so you have ten 1½ × 4-inch rectangles. Halve each piece horizontally—you now have 20 rectangles, each 1½ × 4 inches. Build up each miniature layer cake using three rectangles of cake (you'll have two leftover pieces) and sandwich each layer with the frosting. Spread frosting over the tops, sprinkle with the chopped pecans, and serve.

Maraschino Cookies

Raspberry Custard Tarts

Dreaming

H. Scott.

WORDS BY
ANTHONY STEPHAN
MUSIC BY
MIGUEL

Red Velvet Layer Cakes

The moments spent sharing cocktails and laughing with your girlfriends will live on in your heart forever. On this incredibly special occasion, these cocktails really do take to the stage and sing out to be tasted. Be creative with your friends' favorite drinks and flavors. My favorite drink is champagne, and adding a heart-shape ice cube of any flavor really makes it special! For those who like the taste of cherries, my Devil Drinks Martini cocktail is delicious. And why not take it one note higher with the Chocolate-Covered Cherry Martini?

THE DEVIL DRINKS MARTINI

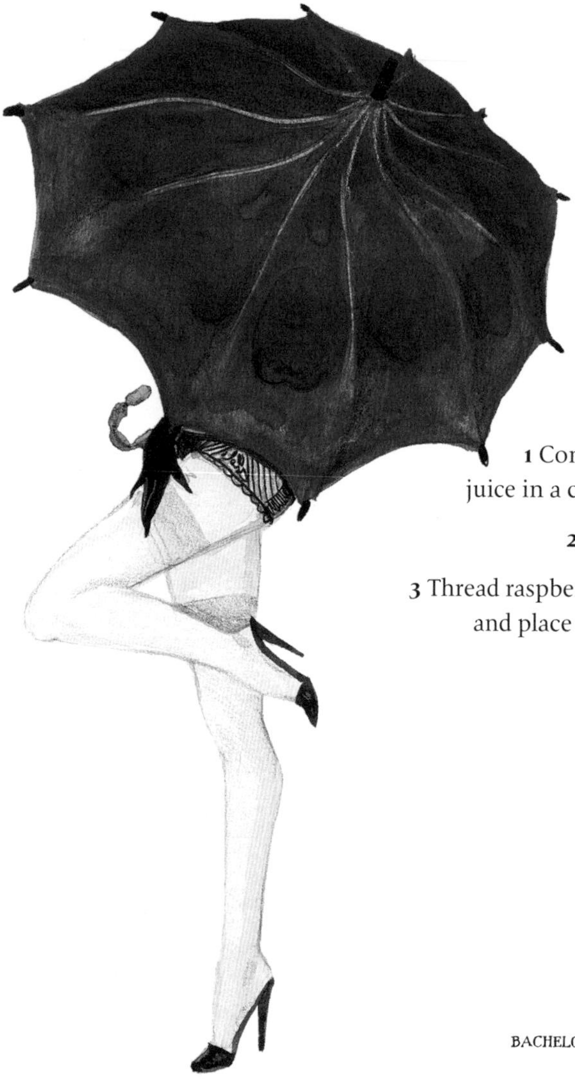

5 ice cubes
2 tablespoons black vodka
2 tablespoons cherry juice
raspberries and blueberries,
to decorate

1 Combine the ice cubes, vodka, and cherry juice in a cocktail shaker; shake for 5–10 seconds.

2 Pour the mixture into a martini glass.

3 Thread raspberries and blueberries onto a toothstick and place them in the drink. Serve immediately.

CHOCOLATE-COVERED CHERRY MARTINI

FOR ALL THREE COCKTAILS:

MAKES **1**

PREP **5** mins

1 tablespoons chocolate syrup

3 maraschino cherries

2 tablespoons chocolate vodka
(use regular vodka if you can't find this)

2 tablespoons cherry vodka

2 tablespoons crème de cacao

1 tablespoon heavy cream

5 ice cubes

1 Swirl the chocolate syrup around inside a martini glass and place the cherries in the bottom of the glass.

2 Pour all the liquids with the ice into a cocktail shaker and shake for 5–10 seconds.

3 Pour the drink into the prepared martini glass. Serve immediately.

HEARTS & CHAMPAGNE

PREP add **3** hours' freezing time for the ice cubes

⅔–1 cup strawberry juice
or other red-colored juice

1 bottle of champagne, chilled

1 A few hours before the party, fill an ice-cube tray that has heart-shape molds with your chosen juice and place it in the freezer until completely frozen.

2 Drop a few frozen hearts into six champagne flutes and top up with champagne. Serve immediately.

The Devil Drinks Martini

Hearts & Champagne

Chocolate-Covered Cherry Martini

If you can imagine drinking a delicious iced vodka with your favorite red juice while watching a ruby sunset on a black night, then you can imagine exactly what this drink has in store for you!

CRANBERRY & VODKA THE BACHELORETTE PARTY WAY

SERVES **1** | PREP **2** mins

5 ice cubes

½ cranberry juice

¼ cup black vodka

1 Place the ice in a glass and pour the cranberry juice over the top.

2 Pour the vodka over the back of a teaspoon into the glass so that it sits on top of the juice and creates a layer of black. Serve immediately.

How to Make a Mini Top Hat

I often find myself in a fabric store being wooed by the exciting products. Lately, my local store started selling hats. I can't help but look, touch, and ask how much (always gulping when I'm told). Our cute top hats are easy to make and, when styled with a fabulous hairdo, are perfect for a night of frivolity.

YOU WILL NEED

✂ pencil ✂ 2 plates—one the size you would like the brim of your top hat to be, the other about 2 inches smaller ✂ 3 sheets of black letter-size card stock ✂ craft knife ✂ cutting mat ✂ glue gun ✂ metal ruler ✂ paper scissors ✂ ½ yard black felt or black felted paper ✂ fabric scissors ✂ ribbons, lace, feathers, or flowers (optional) ✂ comb hair barrette ✂ short piece of thin elastic ✂ needle ✂ hair clip

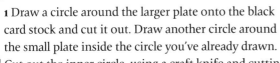

1 Draw a circle around the larger plate onto the black card stock and cut it out. Draw another circle around the small plate inside the circle you've already drawn. Cut out the inner circle, using a craft knife and cutting mat, creating a doughnut-shape piece (piece A).

2 Using more black card stock, form a cylinder (piece B). The mouth of the cylinder should be as big as the inner circle in piece A. Glue the two long edges of the cylinder together. The height of the cylinder depends on how tall you would like the top hat to be.

3 Cut 1¼-inch-long vertical slits around one end of the cylinder, spacing them ½ inch apart, to form flaps.

4 Push cylindrical piece B through doughnut-shape piece A. Bend back the flaps on piece B and secure them to piece A with glue.

5 To make the top of the hat, use the open part of the hat as a template. Draw around it onto the remaining card stock. Draw a larger circle around this one (use the large plate as a template). Cut out the larger circle.

6 Cut short vertical slits, each about ¾ inch long, from the rim inward toward the inner circle, to create flaps. Use this piece (piece C) to cover the hole in the top of the hat, folding over the flaps and gluing them down inside the hat.

7 You can now cover your hat with felt to give it a clean finish and hide all the folded seams. Cut shapes out from the felt, or felted paper, as before, omitting the flaps, and fasten these onto the cardboard hat with a glue gun. At this point you may want to add other decorative details, such as ribbons, feathers, lace, or flowers, to give your top hat a feminine touch.

8 Glue a comb hair barrette on one side underneath the hat so that it can be pushed into the hair.

9 Thread the elastic through the needle. Attach an elastic loop that's no more than ¼ inch long to the hat on the opposite side to the hair barrette by sewing a single stitch onto the hat and tying a knot. Push a hair clip through this to secure the hat in place.

How to Make a Mother-of-Pearl Lamp Shade

On my quest to adopt Britain's lost treasures, I often find beautiful lamp bases with tired old shades, desperate for a style makeover. This shade's new look comes from mother-of-pearl shells, which give it a truly magical glow. I spent months searching the coast for the shells. Actually, that's a lie! You can buy a variety of shells by weight online, so pick them to complement your base.

YOU WILL NEED

✂ working lamp ✂ florist's cellophane ✂ sharp scissors ✂ glue gun ✂ mother-of-pearl shells (the quantity will depend on the size of your shade) ✂ fire-retardant spray ✂ low-wattage lightbulb (25 watts or less)

1 Remove the current cover from your lamp shade, stripping it back to the wire frame.

2 Cover all the panels on the frame with cellophane, creating an invisible base for your shells to sit on. To do this, cut a piece of cellophane that is about 2 inches larger than the panel. Apply glue around the wire edge where you will need to attach the cellophane. Lay the cellophane over the panel, carefully pressing it down from the top to the bottom to make sure it is flat. Use the scissors to cut off the excess cellophane to produce a neat finish that fits the frame perfectly. Repeat this step on all the panels until your lamp shade is entirely covered with cellophane.

3 To cover the lamp shade with the shells, put a small blob of glue on the back of each shell and position it on the cellophane. Working around your shade, start from the bottom and decorate the full circumference of the base with one row of shells, then work your way up the lamp shade. Try to use shells of a similar size in each row to produce an even finish. Overlap each shell slightly to minimize the number of gaps.

4 When the lamp shade is completely covered, carefully check for any obvious gaps and use smaller shells to fill them in. Let the glue dry thoroughly, then spray the entire lamp shade with a coat of fire-retardant spray.

5 Now you're finished and ready to put your beautiful lamp shade back on the lamp base.

NOTE Make sure you use only low-wattage lightbulbs (25 watts or less) with this lamp.

HOW TO CREATE
THE CARMEN MIRANDA

Look to the tantalizing world of cabaret for inspiration for your bachelorette party hairdos. Taking inspiration from the golden age of show girls, with their sparkling costumes and elaborate headpieces and hats, will transform your bachelorette party into a decadent farewell to the bride-to-be's fabulous single days. Carmen Miranda was the poster girl for camp, being flamboyant and an embodiment of the true spirit of carnival! Her outlandish costumes and headpieces wowed American war-time audiences. Use her as your muse for your party preparations and be as creative as you dare.

YOU WILL NEED

🌿 hair mousse 🌿 tail comb 🌿 curling tongs 🌿 hair grips and hairpins 🌿 hat of your choice
🌿 bristle brush 🌿 hairband 🌿 section clips 🌿 hairspray

△ **STEP 1** Curl and set your hair (*see* page 100) to give it a wave. Separate the front central section by making two partings above your eyebrows to meet at the crown. Divide the section across the top of the head into two large pin curls (they don't have to be neat, because they are a base for the hat) and secure the curls with hair grips.

△ **STEP 2** Position the hat and, if needed, use hair grips to secure it.

▽ **STEP 3** Make a diagonal parting from where the crown meets the back of the hat to the front of your ear.

△ **STEP 4** Tease this and smooth the surface with a bristle brush.

△ **STEP 5** Roll this section of hair forward to form a curl at the bottom of the hat, using your thumb to shape the loop. Pin this curl into place.

△ **STEP 6** Make another diagonal parting 2 inches parallel to the first and repeat steps 4 and 5. Repeat steps 3, 4, 5, and 6 on the other side of your head.

△ **STEP 7** Part the remaining hair horizontally 2 inches below the bottom of the hat. Secure the top section with a hairband and clip it out of the way for now.

△ **STEP 8** Sweep the remaining hair upward to meet the ponytail and pin it into place with a horizontal line of hair grips, smoothing the hair with a brush and spraying any flyaway strands into place with hairspray. Divide this section into three and roll each into flat curls at the back of the head, pinning them into place. Leaving the ponytail until last, bring this curl up to meet the bottom of the hat and pin it into place.

WEDDING TEA PARTY

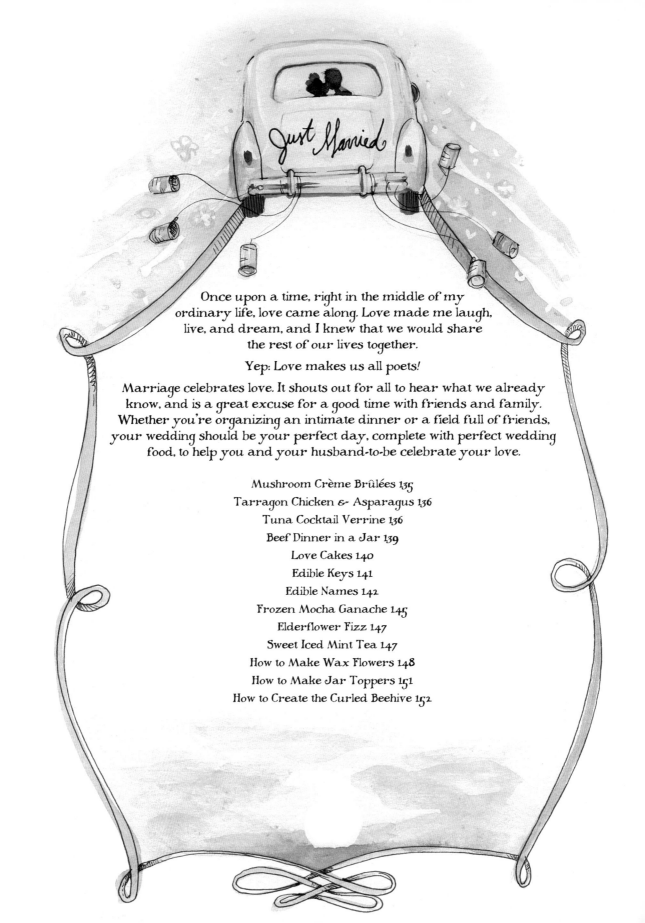

Once upon a time, right in the middle of my ordinary life, love came along. Love made me laugh, live, and dream, and I knew that we would share the rest of our lives together.

Yep: Love makes us all poets!

Marriage celebrates love. It shouts out for all to hear what we already know, and is a great excuse for a good time with friends and family. Whether you're organizing an intimate dinner or a field full of friends, your wedding should be your perfect day, complete with perfect wedding food, to help you and your husband-to-be celebrate your love.

PUT YOUR
PHOTO HERE

The taste of savory custard and a sweet caramel crunch is surprisingly fabulous. Your taste-bud journey begins with sweet, sharp sherry vinegar and finishes with the creamy woodiness of mushrooms. Cooking this dish in old condiment jars is visually enchanting—a great way to begin your wedding meal.

MUSHROOM CRÈME bRÛLÉES

MAKES 6

PREP 20 mins, plus soaking

COOK 1 hour

good handful of dried mushrooms, such as porcini

1 cup milk

⅔ cup heavy cream

4 egg yolks

salt and black pepper

pinch of ground nutmeg

3 tablespoons demerara sugar or other raw sugar

For the garnish

½ cup sherry vinegar

¼ cup granulated sugar

handful of exotic mushrooms

1 Put the dried mushrooms into a bowl. Heat ⅔ cup of the milk in a small saucepan until it is just boiling, then pour it over the mushrooms. Let them soak for at least 1½–2 hours. Keep pushing the mushrooms down under the milk's surface to make sure they all soften.

2 Once the milk has been absorbed, process the mushrooms into a paste in a food processor, then pass this through a strainer. Set aside.

3 Preheat the oven to 250°F. Heat the remaining milk with the cream on the stove to a gentle boil. Take the saucepan off the heat, add the mushroom paste, and beat until the ingredients are well combined.

4 In a separate bowl, beat the egg yolks. Continue to beat as you slowly pour in the mushroom mixture. Season and add the nutmeg.

5 Pour the mixture into six decorative jars, dishes, or small teacups. Place these in a roasting pan and pour hot water into the pan until the water reaches about halfway up the outsides of the jars.

6 Bake for 1 hour or until set (the custards have set if there is a gentle wobble when shaken). Let cool slightly, then sprinkle the demerara or raw sugar over them. Charge up the kitchen blow torch and caramelize the sugar.

7 Meanwhile, for the garnish, heat the vinegar and sugar in a saucepan until reduced to a syrupy sauce. Add the mushrooms and cook for another 3–4 minutes. Place on top of the brûlées.

Serving a creamy dish is a wise move on your wedding day—it solves any "dry chicken" problems and will soak up the wedding fizz!

TARRAGON CHICKEN & ASPARAGUS

SERVES 6
PREP 15 mins
COOK 20 mins

4 tablespoons butter

1¼ pounds chicken breast, cut into ¾-inch cubes

⅓ cup all-purpose flour

1¾ cups whole milk

8 ounces asparagus spears, trimmed and cut into ¾-inch lengths

grated rind of ½ lemon

2 tablespoons chopped tarragon

salt and black pepper

For the crumb topping

1 stick butter, chilled and cubed

1⅔ cups whole-wheat flour, seasoned with salt and black pepper

1 Preheat the oven to 350°F. For the crumb topping, rub the butter into the seasoned flour until clumps form and most of the butter is rubbed in. Spread across a baking sheet and cook for 15–20 minutes, stirring halfway through the cooking time to form big lumps.

2 Meanwhile, melt the butter in a saucepan and add the chicken. Stir and cook for 4 minutes. Sprinkle the flour over the chicken and cook, stirring, for another 3 minutes. Take the pan off the heat and slowly stir in the milk.

3 Return the pan to the heat and bring to a boil, stirring, then add the asparagus, lemon rind, and tarragon and cook for 3–5 minutes, until the sauce thickens to the consistency of lightly whipped cream. Season to taste.

4 Divide the chicken among six plates. Top with the crumb mixture and serve.

Over the years I've attended many weddings, and prawn cocktail appears never to go out of wedding fashion—it's such a crowd-pleaser. I was desperate to find a delicious alternative, and I must thank my good friend Chris for sharing her Asian-inspired tuna cocktail. The flavours and textures of this dish (which is easy to prepare and serve en masse) take you out of this world or, at least, out of this country.

TUNA COCKTAIL VERRINE

SERVES 6
PREP 15 mins, plus chilling

10–12 ounces good-quality raw tuna, cut into ½-inch cubes

juice and grated rind of 3 limes, plus extra grated lime rind to garnish

3 tablespoons sesame seeds, lightly toasted

1 red chile, thinly sliced

3 tablespoons coarsely chopped fresh cilantro

1 tablespoon sesame oil

3 avocados, peeled, pitted and diced

1 cup coconut milk

1 Add the tuna to the lime juice and rind in a large stainless steel bowl and toss them together. Add the sesame seeds, chile, cilantro, and sesame oil and toss the mixture again.

2 Add the avocados and mix them together gently with the other ingredients. Add the coconut milk.

3 Chill the mixture for at least an hour, then put into serving glasses, garnish with a little extra grated lime rind, and serve.

Imagine the scene: It's your big day, the day you may have dreamed about since you were a child; you are surrounded by the people you love; everything is so beautiful and elegant, drowning you in a sea of glamour … What's on the menu? Beef in a Jar, of course! This dish may not be for everyone, but it's tasty and, for me, it represents the bad sense of humor I inherited from my father. Your personality should be part of your big day, so you decide what food you'd like to share with your guests. The best wedding I ever attended served fish and chips in newspaper; can't get better than that, right?!

BEEF DINNER in a jar

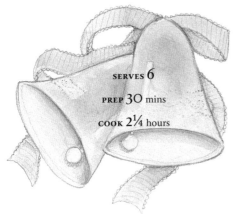

SERVES 6

PREP 30 mins

COOK 2¼ hours

3 tablespoons olive oil

1¼ pounds beef shank, cut into ¾-inch cubes

1 onion, coarsely diced

⅓ cup all-purpose flour

about 2 cups red wine

3 tablespoons tomato paste

3 sprigs of rosemary

4 russet or Yukon gold potatoes, peeled and cut into chunks

salt

1 stick butter

3 tablespoons horseradish sauce

1½ cups trimmed and halved green beans

1 Heat 2 tablespoons of the oil in a large flameproof casserole until hot, then add the beef in batches and brown for 5 minutes. Remove from the casserole with a slotted spoon and set aside. Cook the onion in the remaining oil for 5–7 minutes, until softened.

2 Sprinkle the flour over the onion and cook, stirring, for another 3 minutes. Slowly pour in the red wine while stirring.

3 Return the beef to the casserole with the tomato paste and rosemary. Stir, cover, and simmer for about 2 hours. Occasionally check to stir and make sure the liquid has not all evaporated; add a little more wine, if necessary. Add salt to taste.

4 Meanwhile, boil the potatoes in salted water until tender but not falling apart. Drain and finely mash them with the butter and horseradish sauce. Use a pastry bag to pipe the mashed potatoes into six decorative jars, making sure it's up against the side all the way around the jar.

5 Blanch the green beans for 2 minutes in a saucepan of salted water. Top the mashed potatoes with the beef, then the beans; serve.

Love Cakes

MAKES 16

PREP 20 mins

COOK 50 mins

We recently hosted a Sri Lankan wedding in London.
It was The Vintage Patisserie at its best. Our wedding "favors" were pretty
boxes of traditional Sri Lankan love cake to symbolize fertility, longevity, wealth, health,
and happiness. I was uplifted by this fragrant cake and have adopted it into my family.

1 stick butter, softened,
plus extra for greasing

3 eggs, separated

¾ cup granulated sugar

¾ cup semolina

½ cup cashew nuts, crushed

1 tablespoon rosewater

1 tablespoon honey

1½ tablespoons brandy

½ teaspoon ground cinnamon

½ teaspoon ground cardamom

½ teaspoon ground nutmeg

confectioners' sugar,
for dusting

1 Preheat the oven to 300°F. Grease an 8-inch square cake pan and line the bottom with nonstick parchment paper.

2 Beat together the softened butter, the egg yolks, and granulated sugar. Add the semolina, cashew nuts, rosewater, honey, brandy, and spices.

3 In a grease-free bowl, beat the egg whites until stiff peaks form.

4 Stir a large spoonful of the egg whites into the cake mixture, then fold in the rest, trying to keep as much air in the mixture as possible. Pour the batter into the prepared pan and bake for 50 minutes, until it is golden and firm to the touch and starting to come away from the sides of the pan.

5 Turn off the oven and keep the door ajar to let the cake cool down slowly.

6 Once cool, turn out the cake onto a cutting board and cut into 16 squares. Dust these with confectioners' sugar before putting each into a decorative box.

MAKES
100

PREP
2–3
mins
per key

Rusty old keys excite me.
I wish they could talk so that
I could discover their stories
and secrets. Keys, which unlock
new journeys in our lives, are
so appropriate at a wedding. Use
a silicone key mold (available
online) and follow this recipe
to create your own.

EDIBLE KEYS

1 pound marzipan
edible gold luster spray (available online)

1 Break a small piece of marzipan off the block and press it into a silicone key mold. Using a chocolate scraper, gently scrape the excess marzipan off the mold to create a flat surface.

2 Pull the silicone back at the top of the key so that the marzipan pops out. Gently ease it out of the mold

and transfer it to a baking sheet lined with nonstick parchment paper. Straighten the key, if necessary. Repeat with the remaining marzipan.

3 Let the keys harden overnight, then spray them with edible gold luster.

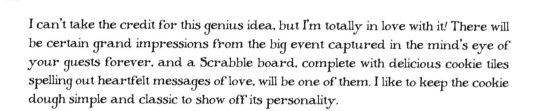

I can't take the credit for this genius idea, but I'm totally in love with it! There will be certain grand impressions from the big event captured in the mind's eye of your guests forever, and a Scrabble board, complete with delicious cookie tiles spelling out heartfelt messages of love, will be one of them. I like to keep the cookie dough simple and classic to show off its personality.

Edible Names

3⅔ cups all-purpose flour, plus extra for dusting

½ teaspoon baking powder

pinch of salt

heaping 1 cup vanilla sugar

2 sticks salted butter, softened

1 egg

¾ teaspoon vanilla extract

½ teaspoon almond extract

For the icing

2 egg whites

3⅔ cups confectioners' sugar, sifted

2 teaspoons lemon juice

1 teaspoon glycerin

store-bought black writing icing or black icing pens

MAKES 50 letters

PREP 1 hour, plus chilling and setting

COOK 10 mins

1 Preheat the oven to 350°F.

2 Mix together the flour, baking powder, and salt in a large bowl. Set the mixture aside.

3 Cream the butter and sugar together with a wooden spoon or an electric mixer until light and fluffy. Beat in the egg and the vanilla and almond extracts. Gradually fold in the flour mixture to form a crumbly dough.

4 Knead the dough, roll into a ball, wrap in plastic wrap, and place in the refrigerator to chill for 30 minutes.

5 Roll out the dough on a lightly floured surface and cut into 50 squares, each the size of a Scrabble tile. Place these on baking sheets lined with nonstick parchment paper and put them in the freezer for 15 minutes to set.

6 Bake the Scrabble tiles for 8–10 minutes, until golden. Let them cool for a few minutes on the baking sheets, then transfer them to a wire rack.

7 To make the icing, beat the egg whites in a large bowl until they become frothy. Beat in the confectioners' sugar a spoonful at a time. Add the lemon juice and glycerin and keep beating until the mixture becomes very stiff and the whites stand up in peaks.

8 If necessary, thin the icing by stirring in a teaspoon of water at a time, until it becomes a good consistency for icing the cookies. Cover the icing with a damp dish towel and let sit for several minutes. Using a small teaspoon, place a blob of icing in the center of a cookie, then gently spread it out across the surface, working out toward the edges, with a toothpick. Repeat for the rest of the cookies. Let the icing set for at least 1 hour.

9 Pipe the letters to spell out the words you will be making onto the squares using black icing and a thin tip, or icing pens. Add the point value for each letter in the corner of the tile for authenticity.

A good wedding meal with speeches can go on for hours and, often, by tea and coffee time (and with plenty of booze under the belt), the guests have left their seats behind and are having a party. Serving Frozen Mocha Ganache is a delicious way to tempt them back to their seats. If you want to offer a choice of flavors, think green jasmine.

Frozen Mocha Ganache

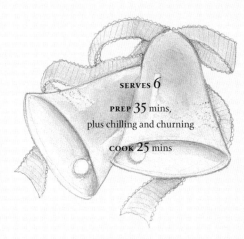

SERVES 6

PREP 35 mins,
plus chilling and churning

COOK 25 mins

8 ounces semisweet chocolate, coarsely chopped

⅓ cup very strong hot coffee (3 double espressos or 2 tablespoons instant coffee mixed with ⅓ cup hot water)

2 cups light cream

1 cup heavy cream

¾ granulated sugar

4 egg yolks

For the ganache

½ cup light cream

2 ounces semisweet chocolate, finely chopped

½ cup heavy cream

1 Break the chocolate into pieces and melt it in a heatproof bowl set over a saucepan of barely simmering water, making sure the bottom of the bowl doesn't touch the water below. Stir in the coffee and set aside.

2 Slowly bring the creams and ½ cup of the sugar to a boil in a heavy saucepan set over low heat, stirring until the sugar dissolves.

3 In a bowl, beat the egg yolks and remaining sugar with a handheld electric mixer set on a high speed until the mixture is thick and pale. Reduce the speed and gradually pour in the hot cream mixture, beating continuously.

4 Return this custard to the saucepan and cook over medium heat, stirring continuously, for 6–8 minutes, until the mixture thickens and coats the back of a wooden spoon.

5 Remove the custard from heat and stir it into the chocolate–coffee mixture. Immediately cover the mixture with plastic wrap, making sure it is flush with the custard's surface to prevent a skin from forming. Let cool, then chill in the refrigerator for 3 hours. Transfer to an ice cream maker and follow the manufacturer's instructions to churn it.

6 Scoop the ice cream into six coffee cups and smooth out the surface. Store the cups in the freezer.

7 To make the ganache, heat the cream and chocolate in a small saucepan set over low heat. Stir continuously until the chocolate has melted, then let the mixture cool.

8 Pour a thin layer of ganache over the ice cream. Put a drop of cream on top, swirl it into a design, then replace the cups in the freezer until 15 minutes prior to serving.

If you can find fresh elderflowers growing on an American black elderberry (*Sambucus nigra* L. ssp. *canadensis*), you can enjoy making your own fizz! Fresh flowers are restricted to summertime, so use dried flower if not available or in doubt of identification, doubling the quantity. The finished product is musky, yet fruity, and easy to drink in copious amounts. For something lighter but equally refreshing, try my Sweet Iced Mint Tea, and for a winter wedding, drink it hot!

ELDERFLOWER FIZZ

MAKES 6 bottles
of varying sizes

PREP 15 mins,
plus soaking and maturing

EQUIPMENT

large 1-gallon container

zester

liquid measuring cup

strainer

funnel

sterilized jars

2½ cups compressed elderflowers

3⅓ cups granulated sugar

zested rind and juice of 2 lemons

2 tablespoons white wine vinegar

1 Mix the elderflowers with 17 cups (1 gallon) of water and stir thoroughly. Add the sugar and stir it until most of it has dissolved. Add the lemon rind and juice and the vinegar. Cover the container and let it stand in a warm place for 24 hours.

2 Strain the liquid and pour it into sterilized jars.

3 Let the jars stand for two weeks in the refrigerator, checking them daily to make sure the jars are not too full. If they are, gently release some of the gas. Consume the drink within one month.

SWEET ICED MINT TEA

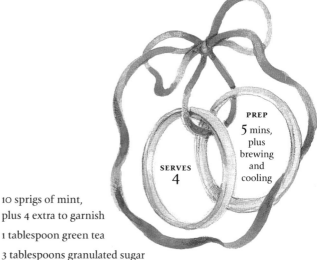

PREP 5 mins, plus brewing and cooling

SERVES 4

10 sprigs of mint, plus 4 extra to garnish

1 tablespoon green tea

3 tablespoons granulated sugar

1 Boil 4 cups of water. Pour a small amount into a teapot and swish it around to warm the pot, then discard.

2 Combine the mint, green tea, and sugar in the teapot, then fill it with the rest of the hot water. Let the tea brew, stirring the leaves once or twice, for 3 minutes.

3 Pour the tea through a tea strainer into teacups and let cool. Garnish with the remaining mint sprigs.

How to Make
Wax Flowers

You can capture a fresh flower's beauty and make it last by using a simple waxing technique, and your guest can take home a floral tribute to the day. Some of the best flowers to use are roses, daisies, thistles, tulips, hyacinths, and other flowers that have a natural waxy coating. Leaves and hardy plants always wax well, so don't be afraid to try out a selection—just avoid very delicate flowers that will wither in the heat of the wax.

YOU WILL NEED

🖋 bowl 🖋 paraffin wax 🖋 saucepan 🖋 disposable wooden stick or skewer for stirring the wax 🖋 thermometer 🖋 nonstick parchment paper 🖋 selection of fresh, firm flowers and leaf clusters 🖋 scissors 🖋 jar filled with water 🖋 bowl of iced water 🖋 container in which to arrange the display

1 Fill a glass bowl three-quarters full with paraffin wax and set it over a saucepan of barely simmering water, making sure the bottom of the bowl doesn't touch the water below. Use a wooden stick or skewer to stir the paraffin until it becomes liquid. Put your thermometer into the wax and keep it there—you need to get it to 130–140°F and maintain it.

2 Lay out a sheet of nonstick parchment paper over an area of your work surface.

3 Clip the flower stems 5 inches below the calyx and set them in a jar of water. Clip and set aside a selection of attractive leaf clusters.

4 Hold a flower upside down by its stem and dip it into the warm wax without letting the flower touch the side of the bowl. Hold the flower in the wax for 2–3 seconds. Remove the flower, gently shake off any excess wax, then dip it into a bowl of iced water and lift out. Place your flower on its side on the parchment paper for about 5 minutes to harden completely. Once the wax has hardened, gently hold the flower head and dip the stem in and out of the wax to coat the entire flower. Repeat the same process with all the flowers and leaves. If you're waxing a flower that has many petals, spoon wax into the center of the flower after dipping to make sure of complete coverage.

5 Once you're happy with your flowers, they can be used to create a beautiful and lasting display.

How to Make
Jar Toppers

Jars are one of the things I like to collect that actually have a use. I've often covered jar lids in fabric and added a pretty label to give homemade preserves and other stuff as gifts. A few years ago, when I rediscovered my glue gun, I went a little crazy and glued everything to everything! And jars—you don't get away! Whatever your occasion, this is a fantastical way of adding the personal touch to a jar of something delicious.

YOU WILL NEED

✄ selection of empty glass food jars with screw-on lids ✄ selection of themed jar toppers ✄ glue gun ✄ newspaper or scrap paper ✄ spray paints in celebratory colors, such as red, gold, green, and silver

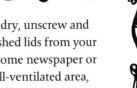

1 Collect some empty food jars with screw-on lids—a selection of varying shapes and sizes makes an attractive display. When you are happy with your jars, make sure they are thoroughly washed and dried.

2 Find some items to use as jar toppers—old Christmas decorations or collected pinecones work well. For weddings, you can find themed toppers in cake shops.

3 Next, use a glue gun to glue a topper to each of your jar lids. Let them dry.

4 When completely dry, unscrew and remove the embellished lids from your jars, sit the lids on some newspaper or scrap paper in a well-ventilated area, and spray the lids and their toppers with the spray paints. Spray a little at a time, coming back to add more coats, if necessary (this avoids any unwanted clumps of paint).

5 When the lids and their toppers are dry and you are happy with the finish, simply fill the jars with treats, drinks, dinners … anything you like!

HOW TO CREATE THE
CURLED BEEHIVE

Just as important as your dress is your wedding-day hair and makeup. With so much choice for vintage hair inspiration, whether you are using a hair stylist or doing it yourself, it's really worth investing time in finding your perfect hairstyle for the big day. Our advice is to stick to your preferred style decade and just go for it! Our model for this look is a true 1960s belle, so embracing that, along with the timeless chic of the era, we present "The Curled Beehive."

YOU WILL NEED

hair mousse ✇ tail comb ✇ heated rollers ✇ section clips ✇ hair rat, if your hair is too fine to create a structured beehive (available in pharmacies and online) ✇ bristle brush ✇ hairpins and grips ✇ hairspray ✇ decorative hair barrettes, flowers, or jewels

◁ **STEP 1** Curl and set your hair with heated rollers for a loose wave (*see* page 100). Make sure the rollers at the front and center of the head are rolled backward to create as much volume as possible. If you have bangs, style it at this stage.

▷ **STEP 2** Remove the rollers and section the hair from ear to ear across the head. Divide the front section into three with two partings above each brow. Make sure each section is the same size.

◁ **STEP 3** If using a hair rat, attach it now. Take a handful of hair from one side of the head, just behind the parting, and tease and smooth it, then sweep it to the opposite side of the head (over the hair rat, if using). Secure with pins in a vertical line down the middle of the head.

▷ **STEP 4**
Repeat step 3 on the other side and pin to create the base of the beehive. Spray with hairspray to secure.

◁ **STEP 5**
Working on the front sections one at a time, repeat steps 3 and 4, teasing the hair from behind and smoothing the strands backward with a bristle brush, to pin the hair securely over the beehive.

▷ **STEP 6** Using the hair at the back of the head, loop sections up to create pin curls that meet the beehive. Secure with hairpins. We have left some hair loose for a soft, feminine look, but this style works just as well with all the hair pinned up off the neck. Decorate the beehive with chic barrettes, flowers, or jewels.

Nature's most romantic gift is certainly a baby.
Life takes on new meaning and direction on the birth
of a child. Friends and family await the announcement of
the birth with anticipation, eager to bear love and gifts. Everyone
wants to care for mom-to-be and show her how special she is to be bringing
a new person into the world. Baby showers have become increasingly
popular in Great Britain, borrowing the occasion from you, our friends
over the pond. A baby shower is a celebration of a pregnancy and
impending birth, in which the mom-to-be, at center stage, is showered with
gifts from her friends for the soon-to-be-born baby. My uberglamorous
take on the occasion celebrates the very special mom-to-be in style, and
surrounds her with loved ones, delicious food, and plenty of laughter.

thank you

Tarte Tatin excites me on many levels. First, the variety of flavors you can play with is endless. I love this savory version with sweet roasted peppers, zucchini, and a kick of Parmesan— it's truly heavenly! Second, I love the suspense of not seeing the finished product until the end. Allow yourself time to arrange the vegetables in pretty spirals; do this early in the day and add the pastry when your guests arrive, so you have more time to relax.

MiNi Savory Tarte Tatin

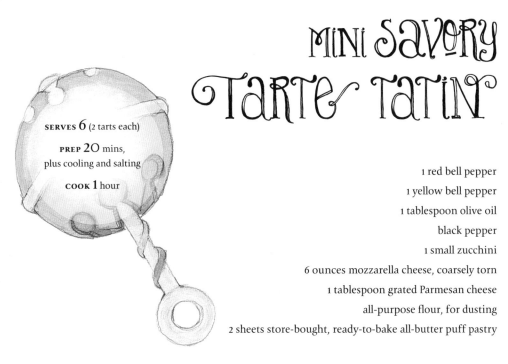

SERVES 6 (2 tarts each)

PREP 20 mins, plus cooling and salting

COOK 1 hour

1 red bell pepper

1 yellow bell pepper

1 tablespoon olive oil

black pepper

1 small zucchini

6 ounces mozzarella cheese, coarsely torn

1 tablespoon grated Parmesan cheese

all-purpose flour, for dusting

2 sheets store-bought, ready-to-bake all-butter puff pastry

1 Preheat the oven to 375ºF.

2 Place the bell peppers in a baking pan, drizzle them with the oil, sprinkle over some salt, and roast them for about 45 minutes, until the skins are nearly black. Remove the peppers from the oven, place them in a plastic food bag, seal the bag, and set it aside for about 30 minutes to cool (this makes it easier to remove the skins). When they have cooled down, peel the roasted peppers and cut them into strips about ½ inch wide.

3 Using a vegetable peeler, slice the zucchini lengthwise into ribbons that are just thin enough to roll up. If they are too thin to roll properly, use a knife to slice the zucchini to the right thickness. Place the zucchini ribbons on a plate, sprinkle them with salt, and set

aside for 20 minutes. Then wash the zucchini ribbons under cold running water and dry on paper towels.

4 Roll a strip of roasted pepper inside a ribbon of zucchini, trimming them to the same width, and put two rolls in each of the cups of a 12-cup shallow muffin pan (its cups should be about 2½ inches in diameter). Sprinkle with the mozzarella and Parmesan cheeses.

5 Roll out the pastry on a floured work surface to a thickness of about ¼ inch. Using a round pastry cutter that's about ½ inch wider than the cups of your pan, stamp out 12 circles. Gently press a circle over each cup. Bake for 15–20 minutes, until the pastry is puffed up and golden. Serve with a grinding of black pepper.

Apart from my nan's chicken soup, pea and ham is top of the comfort-soup chart for me—and it's incredibly simple to make! Personally, I don't think about seasoning until the end, because the ham hock itself is salty, so the dish often needs no extra salt. Serve this soup with homemade Scone Rarebit (see opposite) in simple teacups, and you can't help but make people happy.

Pea & Ham Soup

SERVES 6

PREP 10 mins

COOK 1½ hours

1¼ cups green split peas
1 small onion, chopped
1 celery stick, chopped
1 small leek, chopped
1 small carrot, chopped
1 large garlic clove, crushed
1¾-pound small ham hock
salt and black pepper
Scone Rarebit, to serve (see opposite)

1 Place all the ingredients except the seasoning in a large saucepan and cover with water. Bring up to a boil and simmer for 1½ hours. During this time, skim off any foam that rises to the surface and top up the water as necessary to make sure everything remains covered with water.

2 Remove the ham hock, then blend the liquid using a handheld blender or food processor to create a smooth soup. Season the soup with salt, if needed, and black pepper.

3 Cut the ham off the bone and return it to the soup. Serve the soup with a helping of Scone Rarebit.

Don't you just love it when two British classics come together in perfect harmony? Scones—a sweet version of your biscuits—are essential to any afternoon tea, and they are truly delicious transformed into rarebit and served with Pea and Ham Soup.

Scone Rarebit

MAKES **12**

PREP **20** mins

COOK **25–30** mins, plus cooling

1⅔ cups white bread flour, plus extra for dusting

1 tablespoon baking powder

pinch of sea salt

4 tablespoons butter, diced, plus extra for greasing

2 tablespoons thyme leaves

½–⅔ cup milk, plus extra for brushing

For the rarebit

1 tablespoon butter

2 tablespoons all-purpose flour

⅔ cup ale

1⅓ cups sharp cheddar cheese

1 teaspoon Dijon mustard

1 tablespoon Worcestershire sauce

1 egg yolk

1 To make the scones, preheat the oven to 400°F. Lightly grease a baking sheet.

2 Sift the flour, baking powder, and sea salt into a bowl. Rub the butter into the flour mixture until it resembles fine bread crumbs. Stir in the thyme leaves.

3 Using a knife, gradually cut in just enough of the milk to make a soft dough.

4 Roll out the dough on a lightly floured work surface to a thickness of ½ inch. Using a pastry cutter, stamp out 12 circles with a diameter of 2¼ inches.

5 Place the circles on the prepared baking sheet. Brush with milk and bake for 12–15 minutes. Transfer the scones to a wire rack to cool.

6 To make the rarebit, first melt the butter in a saucepan and add the flour. Cook for 2 minutes, stirring, then take the pan off the heat and add the ale, stirring continuously. Return the pan to the stove and gently bring the liquid to a simmer, stirring continuously. Let it simmer for 3 minutes, then remove the pan from the heat again and add the cheese, mustard, and Worcestershire sauce. Let the mixture cool for a few minutes, then whisk in the egg yolk.

7 Preheat the broiler to high. To assemble the rarebit, cut the scones in half, place them on a baking sheet, and add a dollop of rarebit mixture on top of each half. Broil the scones for about 3 minutes, until they are deliciously golden and bubbling.

At a gathering of girls I often find these dips to be the most popular of all the food offered. I have got through gallons of hummus, breads and crudités at baby showers, and would simply need to remortgage my property if I were to buy them each time. Dips and breads are simple and cheap to make, and they won't fail to hit the spot. Tailor the flavors to your group's tastes and don't mention how easy it is to make the flatbreads; your guests won't believe you!

Dip Delight with Homemade Flatbreads

Chunky Beetroot Dip

1 cup grated, cooked beets (about 3 whole beets)

1 tablespoon horseradish sauce

¼ cup crème fraîche or sour cream

1 Simply mix together all the ingredients and serve!

SERVES 6 as a trio of dips
PREP 40 mins, plus chilling and proving
COOK 40 mins

Baba Ghanoush

1 large eggplant

1 teaspoon olive oil

2 small garlic cloves, crushed

3 tablespoons tahini

1 tablespoon lemon juice

¼ cup extra-virgin olive oil

salt and black pepper

1 Preheat the oven to 400°F. Place the eggplant on a baking sheet, rub the 1 teaspoon olive oil over it, and bake for 30–40 minutes, or until the flesh is soft. Let it cool slightly.

2 Carefully peel and discard the eggplant skin. Blend the flesh with the garlic, tahini, lemon juice, and extra-virgin olive oil in a food processor until smooth. Season the dip to taste before serving.

Avocado Hummus

1 avocado, peeled and pitted

1 (15-ounce) can chickpeas, rinsed and drained

½ onion, chopped

2 large garlic cloves

1 tablespoon lemon juice

1 teaspoon ground cumin

salt and black pepper

1 Blend all the ingredients in a food processor, put the hummus into a bowl, cover with plastic wrap, and refrigerate for at least 1 hour before serving.

Flatbreads

½ teaspoon salt

1 tablespoon extra-virgin olive oil

2 cups all-purpose flour, plus extra for dusting

1 Dissolve the salt in ½ cup lukewarm water, then add the oil. Add the water mixture slowly to the flour, kneading the mixture until the dough is smooth. Cover with a clean, dry cloth and set aside for 30 minutes.

2 Roll out walnut-size pieces of the dough thinly on a floured surface into 4 × 2-inch flatbreads. Cook each piece in a dry skillet for 3 minutes per side, then serve them with your delicious dips!

At the mention of this British dessert, my mind races through the various references to fools, from the fool that accompanied King Lear on his journey across the howling heath, to the modern question "What kind of fool are you?" But the name of this delicate dessert actually comes from the French word *fouler*, meaning to press or crush, referring to the crushed fruits that are gently folded into thick cream. It is this simplicity that makes the dish shine. And as the British fool, I get to choose the berries and sing "here we go round the mulberry bush" as I dish up!

GREAT BRITISH FOOL

SERVES 6

PREP 5 mins, plus chilling

COOK 10–15 mins

1 cup heavy whipping cream

1 tablespoon confectioners' sugar

1 cup fruit compote

For the compote

1 pound seasonal fruit (such as blackberries, raspberries, gooseberries, or rhubarb), trimmed

2½ tablespoons granulated sugar

couple of splashes of elderflower or ginger syrup (optional)

1 To make the compote, preheat the oven to 350°F.

2 Place the fruit in a large saucepan and sprinkle with the sugar. Add enough water to just cover and gently bring the mixture to a boil, letting the sugar dissolve. Let the mixture simmer for 10–15 minutes, until the fruit has completely softened.

3 Add the syrup, if using (elderflower works very well with gooseberries, and ginger is great with rhubarb). Check the compote for sweetness and add more sugar, if you desire. Let the compote cool, then chill in the refrigerator for 30 minutes.

4 Whisk the cream and confectioners' sugar together until soft peaks form (it should not be too thick), then fold in the compote. Divide the fool among six decorative glasses and serve.

It would be rude not to have chocolate at a mother-to-be's tea party, and these gracious, gently baked cheesecakes should extract all the right sounds from your guests. I love cooking them in old makeup sets for an elegant touch. Add a sprinkle of chocolate shavings at the end to really lift the dish.

MINI BAKED CHOCOLATE CHEESECAKES

MAKES 6

PREP 20 mins, plus chilling

COOK 35 mins

2 ounces semisweet chocolate, plus ½ ounce chopped semisweet chocolate and extra shavings to decorate

4 tablespoons unsalted butter

1 cup crushed graham crackers

½ cup cream cheese

2 tablespoons granulated sugar

⅓ cup sour cream

2 eggs, beaten

1 tablespoon unsweetened cocoa powder

1 teaspoon vanilla extract

1 Preheat the oven to 350°F. Break the 2 ounces of chocolate into pieces and melt it in a heatproof bowl set over a saucepan of barely simmering water, making sure the bottom of the bowl doesn't touch the water below. Let the melted chocolate cool to room temperature.

2 Melt the butter in a saucepan and mix in the crushed graham crackers. Divide the mixture equally into six and press one portion into the bottom of each of your dishes or teacups (which should be at least ½ inch high).

3 Mix the cream cheese and sugar until smooth, then add the sour cream, eggs, cocoa, vanilla extract, and melted chocolate. Mix well, then fold in the chopped chocolate. Pour this mixture into the dishes over the cookie crusts. Place the cups in a large baking pan and add enough water to the pan to reach halfway up the outsides of the cups. Cook for 30 minutes, until firm to the touch. Chill for at least an hour and until ready to serve.

A tasty tea cozy for a hot ginger drink! Lifting box lids to reveal what's underneath is one of life's simple pleasures. This hot-drink topper evokes that feeling and, what's more, it's delicious, crunchy, and perfect to dip into your Ginger Syrup Tea (see page 172).

CINNAMON TEA COZIES

MAKES 6
PREP 45 mins, plus chilling
COOK 12–15 mins

2 cups all-purpose flour, plus extra for dusting

1 tablespoon ground cinnamon

½ teaspoon salt

1 stick butter, softened

½ cup granulated sugar

1 teaspoon vanilla extract

1 egg, beaten

For the topping

¼ cup superfine sugar or granulated sugar

½ teaspoon ground cinnamon

1 Sift the flour, cinnamon, and salt into a bowl, then rub in the butter until the mixture resembles bread crumbs. Add the sugar and vanilla and mix into a stiff paste, then mix in the egg to form a dough. Knead on a lightly floured surface until smooth. Wrap in plastic wrap and refrigerate for 30 minutes. Preheat the oven to 350°F. Line a baking sheet with nonstick parchment paper.

2 Divide the dough into two pieces (A and B). Roll out each piece into a large rectangle and cut it into strips about ¼ inch wide. On piece A, fold every other strip all the way back over itself. Lay a strip from B over the area on piece A with the gaps, perpendicular to the piece-A strips, placing it close to the line where you folded the strips from piece A back. Now unfold the strips from piece A, laying them over the strip from piece B. Next, fold back the strips from piece A that you didn't fold

last time and lay down the next strip from piece B, positioning it as close as possible to the first strip from piece B. Repeat this pattern until you have used all the strips from B and have created a lattice structure. Use a pastry cutter that is just bigger than your teacups to cut out six circles from the lattice. Put these onto the baking sheet. (If you have a ramekin that's the same size as your teacups, upturn it, cover it with a square of nonstick parchment paper, lay the toppers over that, and gently push the edges of the pastry circles over the edge of the ramekin bottom to create a lip—you'll need to cut your circles ¾ inch larger than your teacup, in this case. You can bake the cookies on the ramekins.)

3 Bake for 12–15 minutes, until golden brown. As soon as the toppers come out of the oven, shake a mixture of the superfine sugar and cinnamon over them and let cool.

Some may argue that this is not a traditional afternoon teacake and, actually, they would be right. With this out of the way, and copious amounts of tea to be drunk, this cake oozes zesty orange and is perfect with a cup of tea! Ground almonds are my secret weapon to increase levels of scrumptiousness.

ELDERFLOWER & ORANGE
AFTERNOON TEACAKE

SERVES 10–12
PREP 15 mins
COOK 45–50 mins

1½ sticks softened butter, plus extra for greasing

¾ cup superfine sugar or granulated sugar

3 eggs

1¼ cups all-purpose flour

1 cup ground almonds (almond meal)

1¾ teaspoons baking powder

½ cup milk

For the elderflower drizzle

¼ cup elderflower syrup

grated rind of 1 orange

¼ cup granulated sugar

1 Heat the oven to 325°F. Grease and line a 9 × 5 × 3-inch loaf pan with a strip of nonstick parchment paper that overhangs the pan.

2 Cream the butter and sugar together with a wooden spoon or an electric mixer until light and fluffy. Beat in the eggs, flour, ground almonds, baking powder, and milk until the batter is smooth. Pour it into the prepared pan. Bake for 45–50 minutes, until the cake is golden and a toothpick that's inserted into the center comes out clean.

3 Meanwhile, heat the drizzle ingredients over medium heat for 5 minutes, until the sugar dissolves and the drizzle takes on the flavor of the rind. Set aside until the cake is ready.

4 As soon as the cake is cooked, using the overhanging paper, turn it out of the pan onto a wire rack, prick it all over with a toothpick, and pour the drizzle over the it. The pieces of orange rind will stick to the top for a lovely burst of color. Let the cake cool, then slice and serve.

Cinnamon Tea Cozies

Ginger Syrup Tea

Elderflower & Orange Afternoon Teacake

Tea for most is like a warm hug. It brings us together and opens our souls to beautiful conversations. Drinking tea during pregnancy must be done with care. Caffeinated tea should be taken in moderation, yet Ginger Tea is not only delicious but is good for nausea. So ladies, drink your pregnant heart out, and if you need something cold, add sparkling water for a ginger sizzler!

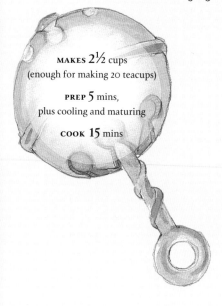

MAKES 2½ cups
(enough for making 20 teacups)

PREP 5 mins,
plus cooling and maturing

COOK 15 mins

GiNGeR SYRUP Tea

3-inch piece fresh ginger (about 3½ ounces), unpeeled
1 cup granulated sugar
2 cups noncarbonated water

To serve cold
sparkling water
ice cubes
lime wedges

1 Add the ginger, sugar, and water to a saucepan. Bring to a boil over low heat, letting the sugar dissolve. Raise the heat and let the mixture simmer for 10 minutes.

2 Remove from the heat and let the mixture cool to room temperature. Strain, and keep refrigerated for up to two weeks.

3 To serve cold, put about 2 tablespoons of the syrup in a glass and top up with sparkling water, ice, and a lime wedge. Stir gently.

4 To serve hot, top up with hot water for that cozy tea! Stir gently.

Jeweled Red Jasmine Tea

Add 1 bulb of Blooming Tea Thousand Year Red (available online)
to each cup of tea and top up with hot water as needed!

HOW TO MAKE
VINTAGE-MOTIF BABY HANGERS

Looking back at my baby pictures, I can see I had some fantastic outfits. My mom gave them to her best friend when she was pregnant, which I totally understood, but I would not have minded if she'd kept my cute sailor's dress, my Minnie-Mouse outfit (including ears), and my baby fur coat. If she had, I would have made these hangers and had my favorite pieces on show.

YOU WILL NEED

✄ cream, blue, and pink matte water-base paint (use small samples sizes) ✄ paintbrush ✄ wooden hangers ✄ vintage and vintage-style printed images for the motifs ✄ craft knife ✄ cutting mat ✄ glue stick ✄ clear matte wood varnish

1 Paint all your hangers in your chosen colors (you may need two or three coats). Let the hangers dry between coats. It will be easiest to paint one side at a time, letting it dry before turning it over to paint the other side.

2 Cut out your motifs carefully using a craft knife. Take your time to make sure you have a neat finish. Then glue the motifs into place on your hangers.

3 Let the glue dry for 10–15 minutes, then paint a coat of clear varnish over the hanger, including over the motif. Depending on the type of varnish used, it may look better to apply a couple of coats to achieve an even coverage. Let dry between coats. After the final coat is dry, your cute vintage motif hangers will be ready to show off some adorable baby clothes.

HOW TO CREATE THE CHEESECAKE

The 1950s was the decade of the baby boomers, so we've drawn inspiration from this era for the perfect baby shower hairdo! Having kept the country going while the men were away fighting World War II, many women were spending more time at home in the 1950s. Practical workplace hairstyles were abandoned in favor of fuller, softer looks. This daring, glamorous Cheesecake pin-up style reveals the neck, which is quite appealing during pregnancy, I'm told!

YOU WILL NEED

❧ hair mousse ❧ tail comb ❧ curling tongs and bobby pins or curl clips, or heated rollers ❧ section clips ❧ bristle brush ❧ hairspray ❧

◁ **STEP 1** Curl and set your hair (*see* page 100), using curling tongs or heated rollers. Once the hair has cooled, remove the grips or clips or rollers and part the hair across the head from ear to ear. Then divide the front section into three by parting the hair above both eyebrows.

◁ **STEP 2** Starting with the front section, tease at the hairline, working your way about halfway down the length of the hair. Then smooth the top of this section, working from the back with a bristle brush. Spray liberally with hairspray.

◁ **STEP 3** Using your fingers, roll the front section toward your face, creating a roll, and bring this forward to meet your forehead. You have now created fake bangs! Pin this in place at the back of the roll, then secure the hair at either side with bobby pins. Use your fingers to gently fan out the hair to cover any gaps in the roll and to make it wider.

◁ **STEP 4** Take one of the side sections, tease from behind, and smooth over with the brush. Sweep the hair up and back across the head, securing with hairpins on the top of the head where the fake bangs start. Make sure there is enough volume in this section to disguise any open edges of the front roll. Repeat on the other side.

▷ **STEP 5** Brush the curled hair at the back off your neck and sweep it upward. Pin it into place, forming a horizontal line with the bobby pins all the way around the head, overlapping them to make them secure. Hairspray any flyaway hairs and smooth them with your hand.

◁ **STEP 6** Work on the hair that has just been swept up on top of the head. Pin the curls in place, using their own structure to guide you. This part doesn't need to be neat—this style is soft and feminine.

GENTLEMEN'S TEA PARTY

As a woman, I found this chapter quite daunting to write at
first. I'm not an expert at being a gentleman, nor have I ever been
one. And most of our parties generally involve women. But after the
publication of *The Vintage Tea Party Book*, I was happy to discover that
there was a demand for the material in this chapter. The public asked!
So I've taken guidance from the most dapper of the gentlemen I know
and dug deep into their souls to find out what floats their handsome
boats, while ensuring it all looks enchanting ... the Angel way.

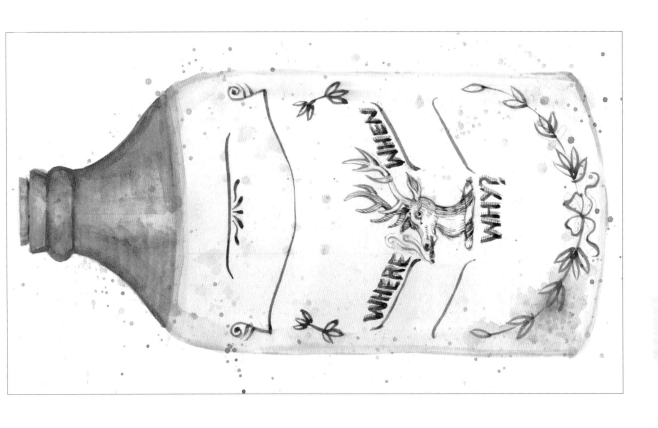

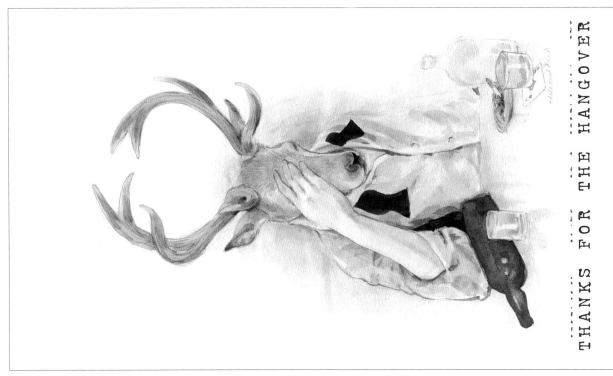

THANKS FOR THE HANGOVER

Crunchy, salty, smoky, sweet, and juicy. These asparagus cigars are simply delectable and you will want to inhale all the flavors just like a real cigar. The good thing is that they are much better for you! They are better served hot while the pastry is still crisp, but I have to admit, they are delicious hours later, too!

Asparagus Cigars

MAKES **12**

PREP **20** mins

COOK **10–12** mins

4 anchovies fillets in oil, drained and chopped

¼ cup light cream

1 tablespoon finely grated Parmesan cheese

1–2 teaspoons lemon juice, to taste

black pepper

6 sheets of 13½ × 12-inch store-bought phyllo pastry, halved

all-purpose flour, for dusting

4 slices of prosciutto, sliced lengthwise into thirds

12 asparagus spears, trimmed, blanched, and drained

olive oil, for brushing

1 Preheat the oven to 400°F. Line a baking sheet carefully with nonstick parchment paper.

2 Grind together the anchovies, cream, Parmesan, lemon juice, and some black pepper to form a paste, using a mortar and pestle.

3 Lay one phyllo rectangle on a lightly floured work surface with a short end nearest to you. (Cover the remaining phyllo with a damp dish towel.) Spread 1 teaspoon of the paste onto a short end of the pastry, lay one piece of prosciutto on top, then an asparagus spear. Brush the pastry with oil and roll it up tightly to enclose the filling. Repeat with the remaining ingredients to make 12 cigars. Transfer to the prepared baking sheet, leaving a ¾–1¼-inch gap between each, and brush with a little more oil. Bake the cigars for 10–12 minutes, until crisp and light golden. Serve immediately.

While on vacation in France, my partner and I ate an unusual steak tartare that oozed with the flavor of curry. We were shocked at how delicious it was and made it our mission to re-create it once back home. We discovered quickly that the steak's delicate flavor must be treated with respect as the star of the dish. So taste the finished dish (oh, if I must), and adjust the flavor by adding a little more of any ingredient as necessary, to get the balance just right. "Yum yum," says Dicky the Fox.

curried STEAK TARTARE

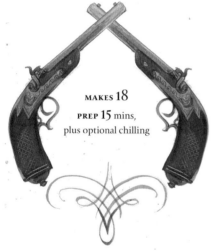

MAKES 18
PREP 15 mins,
plus optional chilling

8 ounces finest-quality steak, finely chopped

1½ ounces shallot, minced

2 teaspoons curry powder

2 teaspoons Worcestershire sauce

6 drops of Tabasco sauce

good pinch of salt and black pepper

flat-leaf parsley, to garnish

1 Mix together all the ingredients except the parsley in a bowl, then form the mixture into 18 lozenges.

2 Either chill, covered, for up to 2 hours, removing from the refrigerator 10 minutes before serving, or serve immediately, garnished with flat-leaf parsley leaves.

Gentlemen's Relish is a strong anchovy paste invented by an Englishman called John Osborne in 1828, who must have been pretty canny, because the recipe is still produced today with a secret license! My dad loves my version spread over toast.

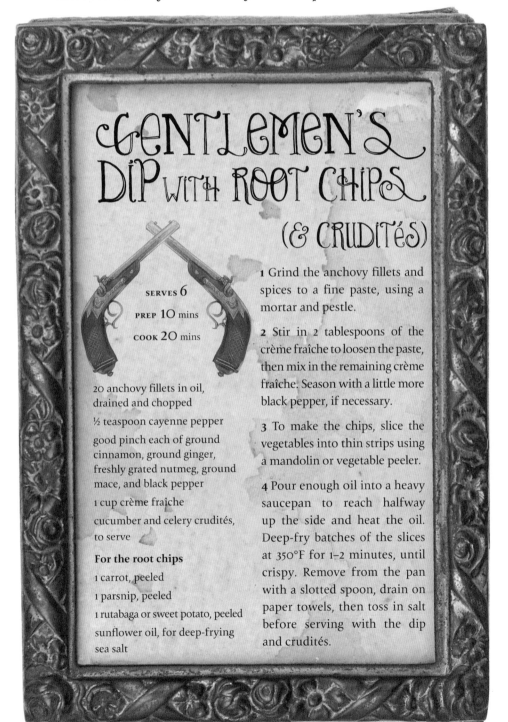

GENTLEMEN'S DIP WITH ROOT CHIPS (& CRUDITÉS)

SERVES 6

PREP 10 mins

COOK 20 mins

20 anchovy fillets in oil, drained and chopped

½ teaspoon cayenne pepper

good pinch each of ground cinnamon, ground ginger, freshly grated nutmeg, ground mace, and black pepper

1 cup crème fraîche

cucumber and celery crudités, to serve

For the root chips

1 carrot, peeled

1 parsnip, peeled

1 rutabaga or sweet potato, peeled

sunflower oil, for deep-frying

sea salt

1 Grind the anchovy fillets and spices to a fine paste, using a mortar and pestle.

2 Stir in 2 tablespoons of the crème fraîche to loosen the paste, then mix in the remaining crème fraîche. Season with a little more black pepper, if necessary.

3 To make the chips, slice the vegetables into thin strips using a mandolin or vegetable peeler.

4 Pour enough oil into a heavy saucepan to reach halfway up the side and heat the oil. Deep-fry batches of the slices at 350°F for 1–2 minutes, until crispy. Remove from the pan with a slotted spoon, drain on paper towels, then toss in salt before serving with the dip and crudités.

Faggots are traditionally made of a mixture of meat scraps shaped into a ball and wrapped in caul (pigs' stomach lining). The caul is visually the best part; it creates a beautiful lacy effect. If you can't get hold of caul, using thin pieces of pancetta is not a bad alternative, trust me!

Freshly cooked squid oozing with garlic butter and chile will send anyone into fishy heaven. When I eat this with my dapper gentleman, he has the tentacles and I eat the body.

Lacy Faggots

MAKES 24

PREP 30 mins

COOK 25 mins

Fishy Trenchermen

MAKES 8

PREP 30 mins

COOK 15–20 mins

4 ounces pigs' liver

4 ounces pork belly

4 ounces pork shoulder

2 ounces bacon

1 cup fresh white bread crumbs

½ onion, finely chopped

handful of chopped parsley

few sage leaves, finely chopped

small sprig of rosemary, finely chopped

pinch of ground mace

½ teaspoon cayenne pepper

½ teaspoon allspice

pinch of salt

pinch of white pepper

12 slices of pancetta

1 Preheat the oven to 350°F.

2 Finely chop the pigs' liver, pork belly, pork shoulder, and bacon and combine them in a bowl. Add all the remaining ingredients except for the pancetta to the meat and mix thoroughly.

3 Shape the mixture into 24 small balls, each about 1¼ inches in diameter. Cut each slice of pancetta in half lengthwise, then in half again widthwise. Use two pieces of pancetta to wrap each faggot so that they cross at the top.

4 Place the faggots on a baking sheet and roast for 25 minutes or until the pancetta is crispy and the pork is cooked through.

2 (1-pound) stale unsliced white country-style loaves

1 stick butter, melted

1 pound baby squid

2 tablespoons olive oil

2 garlic cloves, finely chopped

1 red chile, finely chopped

2 tomatoes, seeded and diced

grated rind and juice of 1 lime

2 tablespoons chopped fresh cilantro leaves

1 Preheat the oven to 350°F.

2 Carefully cut the crusts off the loaves, then cut each loaf into four cubes. Hollow out the cubes with a spoon to make eight bread boxes.

3 Coat the bread boxes inside and out with the melted butter and place them on a baking sheet. Cook for 10–15 minutes, until golden.

4 To prepare the squid, pull out the tentacles and make sure the beak has been removed. Cut the tentacles in half and cut the bodies into three or four small rings.

5 Heat the oil in a skillet set over medium heat and add the garlic. After a few seconds, add the squid, turn up the heat, and flash-fry the squid for 1 minute, tossing it about the pan.

6 Add the chile, cook for a minute, then add the tomatoes. Cook over medium heat for 3 minutes, then add the lime rind and juice and cilantro leaves.

7 Take the skillet off the heat and spoon the mixture into the hollows of the bread boxes, dividing it equally. Serve immediately.

My grandpa is a dapper man. He worked hard all his life in a printing firm in East London and inspired all his children to have great work ethics. He also loves the doughnuts that my granny made for the family. I only found this out recently when researching this chapter. I never knew that when my granny used to make them for the kids, he stood by the fryer chatting so that he could steal some! If they are good enough for my grandpa Don, they are good enough for anyone!

Doughnut balls with
Coffee Cream & Cinnamon Sugar

MAKES 24

PREP 30 mins,
plus proving
and cooling

COOK 40–55 mins

⅔ cup milk

4 tablespoons butter

2 cups white bread flour,
plus extra for dusting

2¼ teaspoons active dry yeast

⅔ cup granulated sugar

2 egg yolks

sunflower oil, for deep-frying and
oiling the bowl

2 teaspoons ground cinnamon

For the coffee cream

2 extra-large egg yolks

⅓ cup superfine or granulated sugar

1½ teaspoons cornstarch

1 teaspoon vanilla extract

2 shots of strong espresso, at room
temperature

1 cup heavy cream

¼ cup skim milk

1 Heat the milk in a small saucepan just to boiling point. Take the pan off the heat, add the butter, and let the butter melt and the milk cool a little. Combine the flour, yeast, and ¼ cup of the sugar in a large bowl. Add the egg yolks to the milk (it should be tepid by now), then add this mixture to the dry ingredients. Combine well, then let sit for a few minutes. Knead on a floured work surface for a good 15 minutes, until smooth and elastic (when you prod the dough it should spring back out). Place in a well-oiled bowl, cover the dough with plastic wrap, and let rise in a warm place for a few hours until almost doubled in size.

2 Take the dough out of the bowl and knock out the air. Shape into 24 small balls, place these on a baking sheet, cover with plastic wrap, and let rise for 30–45 minutes.

3 Put at least a 3¼-inch layer of oil in a deep fryer or a saucepan. Cook the doughnuts, in batches, at 350°F for 2–3 minutes on each side until golden brown. Remove from the oil using a slotted spoon and place on paper towels. Let the doughnuts cool.

4 Mix the remaining sugar with the cinnamon in a bowl, then toss each doughnut in the mixture to coat. Place the doughnuts back on the baking sheet to let them cool for 30–40 minutes.

5 To make the coffee cream, mix the egg yolks, sugar, cornstarch, vanilla extract, and espresso in a small saucepan. Whisk until well combined, then add 2 tablespoons of the cream and heat over medium-high heat, stirring continuously. Mix the milk with the remaining cream and add this to the pan, little by little, stirring continuously, until all the milk has been incorporated. Stir for 5–10 minutes, until the mixture coats the back of a wooden spoon. Remove from the heat and let the cream cool. Set plastic wrap on the surface of the cream to prevent a skin from forming.

6 Put the coffee cream into a pastry bag with a plain tip. Poke a small hole into the side of each doughnut and fill with the coffee cream.

BRANDY SNAPS WITH RHUBARB SYLLABUB

MAKES 12

PREP 30 mins,
plus cooling

COOK 40–50 mins

vegetable oil, for oiling
the spoon (optional)

6 tablespoons butter

⅓ cup superfine or granulated sugar

3 tablespoons light corn syrup

⅔ cup all-purpose flour

2 teaspoons brandy

1 teaspoon ground ginger

½ teaspoon ground cinnamon

finely grated rind of 1 lemon

For the rhubarb syllabub

¼ cup granulated sugar

8 ounces trimmed rhubarb,
cut into ½-inch lengths

generous tot of brandy

1 cup heavy cream

1 Preheat the oven to 350°F. Line a baking sheet with nonstick parchment paper and rub vegetable oil onto the handle of a wooden spoon, or use a silicone spoon of a similar size.

2 Melt together the butter, sugar, and corn syrup in a saucepan. Stir in the flour, brandy, spices, and lemon rind.

3 Drop small spoonfuls of the batter onto the prepared baking sheet, spaced well apart because they will spread in the oven. It is best to cook the snaps in two or three batches so you'll have time to shape them while still pliable.

4 Bake the snaps for 6–8 minutes. They're ready when the batter has spread out into lacy, golden circles. Remove the snaps from the oven and let them cool for a minute before shaping.

5 Use the oiled wooden spoon handle to shape the brandy snaps into cylinders. Let these rest on a wire rack to cool. If the snaps become too brittle to shape, return them to the oven for a minute to soften. Repeat the shaping with the remaining batter.

6 For the rhubarb syllabub, put ¼ cup of water and the sugar in a saucepan and heat until the sugar dissolves. Add the rhubarb, heat until it simmers, then continue cooking for about 15 minutes, until it is soft. Remove from the heat and let cool.

7 Add the brandy and pass the rhubarb mixture through a strainer. Whisk the cream to soft peaks, then gently fold in the rhubarb mixture.

8 Spoon the syllabub into a pastry bag with a plain tip. Pipe into the brandy snaps just before serving.

CHOCOLATE MINT Fudge Pieces

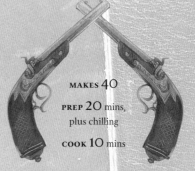

MAKES 40

PREP 20 mins,
plus chilling

COOK 10 mins

12 ounces semisweet chocolate

1 (14-ounce) can condensed milk

2 teaspoons vanilla extract

6 ounces white chocolate

1 tablespoon peppermint extract

2 drops of green food coloring
(optional)

1 Line the bottom of an 8-inch square cake pan with nonstick parchment paper.

2 Melt the semisweet chocolate with ¾ cup of the condensed milk and the vanilla in a heavy saucepan over low heat, stirring continuously. Spread half the mixture over the bottom of the can and chill in the refrigerator for 45 minutes or until firm. Keep the remaining chocolate mixture at room temperature.

3 In another heavy saucepan set over low heat, melt the white chocolate with the remaining condensed milk. Stir in the peppermint extract and the food coloring, if using. Spread this over the chilled layer, then chill for 45 minutes or until firm.

4 Reheat the reserved chocolate to soften, then spread the mixture over the mint layer. Chill for 2 hours or until firm. Cut into 40 rectangles.

Chocolate Mint
Fudge Pieces

Doughnut Balls

Brandy snaps

A whiskey sour is one of the few things other than a beer that one could ask for in order to sound over-the-top masculine, so it would be punishment not to include this recipe here. My male friends love the strong flavors of the bitters, and I do my part by serving up these drinks in attractive old pharmacy bottles. "Honestly, it's not poison!"

WHISKEY SOUR

SERVES 1 | **PREP** 5 mins

2–4 drops of Angostura bitters

¼ cup whiskey

1 tablespoon lemon or lime juice

club soda or lemon-flavored soda

ice cubes

1 Put the bitters in an old pharmacy bottle or glass and add the whiskey and the lemon or lime juice.

2 Stir the drink, then top it up with club soda or lemon-flavored soda and ice cubes.

There are many tales about the invention of the Gimlet, but most include a "Dr. Gimlet," a "Sailor," and a mention of the fact that this sweet-and-sour drink was invented as a cure for something. Hmm …

BASIC GIMLET

SERVES 1 | PREP 1 min

¼ cup gin
2 tablespoons concentrated lime juice
ice cubes

1 Mix the ingredients in a shaker and serve!

HOW TO MAKE A BOW TIE

A gentleman's dapperness depends upon his discreet attention to detail. Anyone can buy a store-bought clip-on tie but, to really impress your peers, make your own. The advantage? You get to match it to your handkerchief, which may match your jacket lining, which may, in turn, match your shoes ... Yes, it's all in the detail!

YOU WILL NEED

✀ measuring tape and ruler ✀ access to a photocopier ✀ large sheet of paper ✀ pencil and thin marker pen ✀ paper and fabric scissors ✀ iron ✀ ½ yard thin iron-on interfacing ✀ ½ yard thin silky patterned fabric for the bow tie (recycling an old cravat works well) ✀ needle and thread to match your fabric ✀ sewing machine

TEMPLATE AT 25 PERCENT ACTUAL SIZE

1 First, if you don't already know your neck size, measure your neck with a measuring tape.

2 Next, photocopy this page at 400 percent and cut out the bow-tie template. Draw around it on a large sheet of paper, extending the middle section to match your measured neck size.

3 Iron the interfacing onto the wrong side of your chosen bow-tie fabric.

4 Lay the template on the wrong side of the bow-tie fabric, on the interfacing, and draw around it with a thin marker pen. Cut out the shape. Repeat this process so that you have two pieces.

5 Lay the two pieces of backed fabric on top of one another, right sides together, and tack around three sides of the bow tie, leaving a narrow end open. Sew the same with your sewing machine, using the edge of the pressure foot as a guide for the seam allowance, then remove the tacks.

6 Turn the bow tie right sides out through the gap (you may want to push a pencil into the corners of the bow tie to give them a nice point). Use a needle and thread to hand sew a tight blanket stitch over the open gap, to close it.

7 Now simply iron your bow tie flat on a low heat and it's ready to wear!

HOW TO TIE A BOW TIE

STREET TEA PARTY

I'm a loud and proud Brit and there's nothing I enjoy more than a good old-fashion street party. Why? Because when our nation gets together and closes off its streets to traffic, throwing them open to the public for a party, there is something pretty spectacular (besides the specific reason for the party itself, of course) to celebrate—and that is the fact that we are a wonderful nation! I'm completely wooed by being part of British history and love everything about the United Kingdom, in all its variety and glory. So, for a street party, I like to cook up a feast using the best British ingredients I can get my hands on, step into my finest British dress, put on my most gorgeous British lipstick, hold my proud British head up high, and have a bloody good time!

Grace your trestle table with the fresh taste of summer. These are my family's simple-but-delicious salads that have fed the masses and will continue to do so! Even as grown-ups we still go to war over the last spoonful of my mom's potato salad!

SERVES
6

TRIO OF SUMMER SALADS

POTATO SALAD

PREP 15 mins | **COOK 15–20** mins

2 pounds new potatoes

salt and black pepper

1 small red onion, finely chopped

3 eggs, hard boiled

⅓ cup mayonnaise

2 tablespoons crème fraîche
or sour cream

good handful of flat-leaf parsley,
chopped, plus extra to garnish

1 Cook the potatoes in lightly salted water for 15–20 minutes, until they are tender. Drain the potatoes and, when they are just cool enough to handle, slice them into circles, quarters, or cubes.

2 Mix together the onion, eggs, mayonnaise, crème fraîche or sour cream, parsley, and some seasoning in a large serving bowl. When the potatoes are still warm but no longer hot, add them to the mayonnaise mixture and gently combine. Serve warm or cold, garnished with parsley.

CHERRY TOMATO SALAD

PREP 15 mins, plus resting

3 cups (about 1 pound) cherry tomatoes of various colors, halved

½ red onion, thinly sliced

salt and black pepper

3–4 tablespoons good-quality extra-virgin olive oil

10 large basil leaves

1 Place the cherry tomatoes in a large serving bowl with the red onion slices. Sprinkle with some salt and black pepper and drizzle with the olive oil. Mix well and taste, adjusting the seasoning if needed.

2 Tear the basil leaves over the salad and mix gently. Let rest for at least 15 minutes to allow for the flavors to mingle, before serving.

COLESLAW

PREP 20 mins, plus chilling

3 cups thinly sliced green cabbage

2 cups shredded carrots

1 Pink Lady, Golden Delicious, or Empire apple, peeled, cored, and thinly sliced

2 shallots, thinly sliced

½ fennel bulb, thinly sliced

½ teaspoon caraway seeds

salt and black pepper

For the dressing

⅓ cup plain yogurt

1 tablespoon cider vinegar

1 teaspoon light brown sugar

⅓ cup mayonnaise

salt and black pepper

1 Combine the yogurt, vinegar, sugar, and mayonnaise in a small bowl and mix well, then season with salt and black pepper.

2 Put all the coleslaw ingredients in a large salad bowl and toss together. Pour the dressing over the coleslaw and toss again. Cover and refrigerate for about an hour. Season with salt and black pepper just before serving.

When feeding a large party, it's important to keep an eye on costs without sacrificing quality. One of my tips is to ask your butcher to debone a good-quality chicken, so you can make sure every last piece is used up. For this recipe, I stuff the chicken with butternut squash, apple, pork, and sage, but you can use whatever takes you prefer. This dish is great thinly sliced and used in sandwiches, or served with salad.

stuffed BRITISH BIRD

SERVES 6–8

PREP 20 mins, plus cooling and resting

COOK 1 hour 20 mins

½ butternut squash, peeled, seeded, and chopped

salt and black pepper

2 tablespoons butter

4-pound whole chicken, deboned (ask your butcher to do this for you)

3 pork link sausages

5 sage leaves, torn

2 tablespoons olive oil

For the applesauce

2 Pippin or McIntosh apples, peeled, cored, and chopped

¼ cup apple juice

1 Preheat the oven to 350°F.

2 Cook the squash in salted boiling water for 15–20 minutes or until tender. Drain and add the butter. Mash, then season to taste. Cool.

3 To make the applesauce, put the apples in a small saucepan with the apple juice and cook over low heat for 10–15 minutes, until soft. You may need to add a little more apple juice to stop the apples from drying out. Cool.

4 Place the bird, skin side down, on a cutting board, level out as much as possible, then season.

5 Spread the squash evenly all over the chicken, then squeeze out the meat from the sausages and place it on top of the squash. Sprinkle the sage leaves over the sausage meat. Finally, spoon the applesauce over the top, then roll up the chicken and truss it with kitchen string.

6 Brush the outside of the bird with the oil and season with salt and black pepper. Put the roll into a roasting pan and cook for 45–60 minutes, until golden brown and cooked through.

7 Remove from the oven and let rest for 10 minutes before slicing.

Potato Salad

Cherry Tomato Salad

Coleslaw

Stuffed British Bird

Thank God for the Earl of Sandwich; without him we would all be eating baguettes! I love to serve classic sandwich combinations with interesting breads that complement the fillings. If I'm watching my pennies, I cut them into triangles to prevent wastage, but I do like to show off by using cookie cutters, like these card-suit ones, which offer a fab way to create cute edible decoration!

MAKES **1** sandwich
of each flavor

PREP **5** mins

BRITISH SANDWICHES

HAM & MUSTARD

butter, at room temperature

2 slices of whole-wheat bread

1 thick slice of ham

English mustard or yellow mustard

1 Butter both slices of bread on one side. Add the ham to one slice, spread some English or yellow mustard on the other slice, and sandwich together. Cut out fancy shapes using cookie cutters.

CHEESE & PICKLE

butter, at room temperature

2 slices of pumpernickel bread

1 thick slice of sharp cheddar cheese

your favorite pickle, chopped, or relish

1 Butter both slices of bread on one side. Lay the cheese on one slice, spread some of the pickle or relish on the other slice, and sandwich together. Cut out fancy shapes using cookie cutters.

FISH STICKS

butter, at room temperature

2 slices of white bread

3 cod fish sticks, cooked

ketchup

1 Butter both slices of bread on one side. Place the fish sticks on one slice, spread some ketchup on the other slice, and sandwich together. You may need to squash down the sandwich before cutting out fancy shapes using your cookie cutters.

SHRIMP COCKTAIL

1 tablespoon mayonnaise

1 teaspoon ketchup

2 ounces cooked and peeled jumbo shrimp

1 sprig of dill, leaves snipped

butter, at room temperature

2 slices of tomato-flavored bread

1 In a small bowl, mix together the mayonnaise and ketchup thoroughly. Add the shrimp and a sprinkling of dill leaves.

2 Butter both slices of bread on one side. Spoon the shrimp mixture onto one slice and sandwich together with the other slice of bread. You may need to squash down the sandwich before cutting out fancy shapes using cookie cutters.

I'm no longer the five year old that tried to eat gelatin through a straw. I'm now a grown woman who tries to. My gelatin salute to the Union Flag (which works for the Stars and Stripes, too) takes time to prepare; each layer needs to set before adding the next. However, when cooking for a large party, you'll probably need to make a few of these gelatins (and I'm sure they will be a hit!), and it takes no more time to make ten than it does to make one!

UNION JACK GELATIN

SERVES
6

PREP
45 mins, plus cooling and chilling

COOK
45 mins

For the blueberry gelatin

1 tablespoon plain powdered gelatin

¾ cup blueberry juice

¾ cup blueberries

For the coconut gelatin

1 tablespoon plain powdered gelatin

1 tablespoon granulated sugar

¾ cup coconut milk

For the raspberry gelatin

1 cup raspberries

1 tablespoon granulated sugar

1 tablespoon plain powdered gelatin

1 To make the blueberry gelatin, place the powdered gelatin in a small saucepan, pour the blueberry juice over it, and let sit for 5 minutes. Set the pan over low heat until the gelatin dissolves; do not let the mixture boil. Then let the mixture cool to room temperature. Once it has, pour it into the bottom of a 2½-cup gelatin mold and put in the refrigerator until the gelatin has set. Once set, sprinkle with the blueberries.

2 Next, make the coconut gelatin. Place the gelatin and sugar in a small saucepan. Pour the coconut milk over it and let sit for 5 minutes. Set the pan over low heat until the gelatin and sugar dissolve; do not let the mixture boil. Once dissolved, let the mixture cool to room temperature, then pour it over the blueberries in the mold. Place in the refrigerator to set.

3 To make the raspberry gelatin, put the raspberries and sugar into a heatproof bowl and cover with plastic wrap.

Rest the bowl over a pan of gently simmering water for 30 minutes so that the juices run out of the fruit.

4 Line a colander with a clean dish towel or a double layer of cheesecloth and pour in the fruit, then set the colander over a bowl. Let the juice drain for about 20 minutes—you may need to gently press the fruit against the side of the colander with a spoon to extract all the juices. Add cold water to the raspberry juice until you have ¾ cup of liquid.

5 Pour the liquid over the gelatin in a small saucepan and let sit for 5 minutes. Set the pan over gentle heat until the gelatin dissolves; do not let the mixture boil. Let the mixture cool to room temperature, then pour it over the coconut gelatin in the mold. Place in the refrigerator until set. Turn out the gelatin onto a serving plate just before serving.

Making rice cereal cakes with my mom is one of my first memories of cooking. I remember being incredibly proud of producing something so heavenly! My seriously cute version brings a little of the British seaside to the table. This fun recipe offers you a very playful way of getting the kids involved in the kitchen, too.

CRISPY PINWHEELS

MAKES 8
COOK 5 mins
PREP 40 mins, plus chilling

3 tablespoons unsalted butter, plus extra for greasing
40 (about 10 ounces) white marshmallows
5 cups puffed rice cereal
red and blue edible color spray (available online)

1 In large saucepan, melt the butter over low heat. Add the marshmallows and stir until they have completely melted. Take the pan off the heat.

2 Add the puffed rice cereal to the pan. Stir until the cereal is well coated.

3 Using a greased spatula, tightly pack the mixture into a greased baking pan that's about 19 × 14¼ inches to achieve a thin but dense layer. Chill in the refrigerator for 30 minutes.

4 Spray the cereal on one side with the red edible color spray, let dry, then remove it carefully from the baking pan. Turn it over, place it on a cutting board, and spray it blue on the other side. Cut the cereal into about 4¾-inch squares.

5 Cut slits into each corner of each square, using a sharp knife, dividing the corners into two. Do not cut all the way to the center of the square.

6 Pick a corner on one square and fold in one half of it, along the slit, toward the center of the square. Squash the tip down at the center. Fold up half of every corner of the square, as shown on the following page, to create a pinwheel. Repeat with the other squares.

STREET TEA PARTY

Shortbread is a classic Scottish cookie that has a delightful snap when broken, and we all expect it to be wonderful and buttery. These little red, white, and blue beauties give you no clue to their Scottish heritage until you taste them, after which you'll be doing the Highland fling!

RED, WHITE & BLUE SHORTBREADS

MAKES 30

PREP 25 mins, plus chilling

COOK 10 mins

1¼ sticks unsalted butter, softened

½ cup confectioners' sugar

1¼ cups all-purpose flour, plus extra for dusting

⅔ cup rice flour or cornstarch

few drops of red and blue food coloring

1 Cream the butter and confectioners' sugar together with a wooden spoon or an electric mixer until light and fluffy. Sift in the flours and mix in. When the mixture forms a ball, knead on a lightly floured work surface for 1–2 minutes, until smooth. Divide into three equal portions. Add a few drops of red coloring to one portion and knead until the color is evenly distributed. Repeat with the blue coloring and another portion of dough.

2 Divide each dough portion in half to have six equal portions: two red, two blue, and two plain. Wrap each in plastic wrap and refrigerate for 30 minutes.

3 Put the doughs on a lightly floured work surface and pat or roll each segment until it's ¼ inch thick. Shape them into similar-size rectangles.

4 Make a stack of these rectangles on a large sheet of nonstick parchment paper, starting with a red layer, followed by a blue layer, and then a plain layer, then repeat the sequence to complete the stack. Cover the dough completely with the paper and wrap it up again in aluminum foil. Chill the dough in the refrigerator for at least 2 hours, until firm.

5 Preheat the oven to 300°F. Remove the dough from the refrigerator and cut the stack into fifteen ¼-inch-thick slices, then cut each of these in half to give you two squares. Place these on a baking sheet about ¾ inch apart and bake on the middle shelf of the oven for 10 minutes or until just tinged with color. Let cool on the baking sheet.

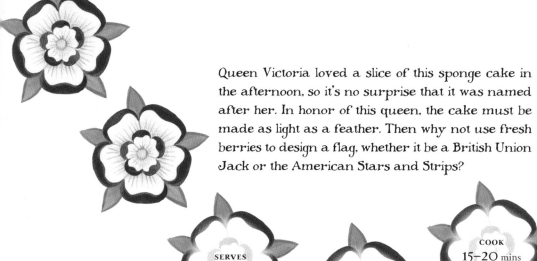

Queen Victoria loved a slice of this sponge cake in the afternoon, so it's no surprise that it was named after her. In honor of this queen, the cake must be made as light as a feather. Then why not use fresh berries to design a flag, whether it be a British Union Jack or the American Stars and Strips?

SERVES 16

PREP 45 mins, plus cooling

COOK 15–20 mins

Victoria Sponge Union Jack

2½ sticks unsalted butter, softened

1⅓ cups plus 1 tablespoon superfine sugar or granulated sugar

5 eggs

2¼ cups all-purpose flour

2¼ teaspoons baking powder

1 teaspoon vanilla extract

raspberries and blueberries (about 4 cups/1 pound each), to decorate

For the buttercream

2 cups confectioners' sugar

2¼ sticks unsalted butter, softened

1 teaspoon vanilla extract

1 Preheat the oven to 350°F. Line the bottom of a 12 × 18-inch rectangular baking pan that is about 1 inch deep with nonstick parchment paper.

2 In a food mixer, cream together the butter and sugar for about 5 minutes, until pale and fluffy. With the mixer set on a slow speed, add the eggs, one at a time, slipping in a tablespoon of the flour about halfway through to stop the mixture from curdling. Sift in the remaining flour and mix until just combined, then stir in the vanilla extract.

3 Transfer the cake batter to the prepared baking pan and spread it with a spoon or spatula to cover the bottom. Bake for 15–20 minutes, until the top is golden and the sponge is springy to the touch. Let cool.

4 Run a knife around the edges of the pan to loosen the cake, then remove it gently from the pan.

5 To make the buttercream, sift the confectioners' sugar into the cleaned food mixer bowl and mix with the butter for at least 5 minutes. Once it is light and fluffy, mix in the vanilla extract.

6 Spread the buttercream over the cake. You do not want to see any cake, because this will form the background of your flag. Then, using the picture opposite as a guide, decorate the cake with the berries to form a Union Jack, or use the berries to make a Stars and Stripes.

Serving delicious drinks at large parties is a hard task without a full bar of mixologists, right? NO! Let me introduce Mr. Punch. He is a big bowl of cocktail normally containing fruit, alcohol, and a mixer. Of course, I like to use British flavors, but you can tailor this to your taste. My biggest tips: Use lemon to preserve freshness and use homemade mixers, such as iced tea, to keep costs down. All that's left is to hold your teacup up and make a toast to all those present, to your loved ones and, of course, to THE QUEEN!

PIMM'S ICED TEA

SERVES 1

PREP 5 mins, plus chilling

ice cubes

⅓ cup Pimm's No. 1

¾ cup brewed Orange Pekoe tea, chilled

1½ teaspoons agave syrup or honey

1½ tablespoons freshly squeezed lemon juice

citrus wedges, mint sprigs, quartered strawberries, and cucumber ribbons, to garnish

1 Fill a highball glass with ice. Add the Pimm's, tea, agave syrup or honey, and lemon juice and stir well. Decorate the drink lavishly.

THYME PUNCH

SERVES 6

⅓ cup superfine sugar or granulated sugar

2 tablespoons freshly squeezed lemon juice

1 cup Hendrick's gin

leaves from 6 sprigs of thyme, coarsely chopped, plus extra to decorate

2¾ cups lemonade

ice cubes

1 Pour the sugar into a pitcher. Add the lemon juice and gin, followed by the thyme. Top up with lemonade, stir, and chill. Just before serving, add a handful of ice cubes and stir again. Decorate the punch with extra thyme.

MEMORABLE BRITISH STREET PARTIES

1919 Peace teas	1981 Wedding of Prince Charles and Lady Diana Spencer
1935 Silver Jubilee of King George V	
1937 Coronation of George VI	2000 The Millennium
1945 VE Day	2002 Golden Jubilee of The Queen
1951 Festival of Britain	2011 Wedding of Prince William and Catherine Middleton
1953 Coronation of Queen Elizabeth II	
1977 Silver Jubilee of The Queen	2012 Diamond Jubilee of The Queen

HOW TO MAKE
ROSETTE BUNTING

Bunting, or a string of flags, which is traditionally made from small triangles of leftover fabric sewn together, makes a great outdoor decoration. I could probably travel the length of Britain on the amount I have made, so for something a little different, I love this take on the classic by using rosettes. It's time-consuming and a bit awkward to do, but the end result is worth it! Decorate the center with something personal or, as I have, with The Queen!

YOU WILL NEED

✄ kettle ✄ dish-washing bowl ✄ 5 regular tea bags ✄ 1 yard royal blue thin cotton fabric

✄ 1 yard white thin cotton fabric ✄ 1 yard red thin cotton fabric ✄ measuring tape ✄

fabric and paper scissors ✄ sewing machine ✄ white cotton ✄ sewing needle

✄ gold card stock ✄ paper and access to a computer and printer ✄ glue stick and glue gun

✄ thin white rope or cord (the length depends on how much bunting you want to make)

1 First, tea stain your fabric to give it an aged look. Boil a saucepan of water several times and fill your dish-washing bowl, then add your tea bags and stir. Add all your fabrics to the water and let sit for at least 30 minutes, then hang the fabrics to dry.

2 When the fabrics are dry, cut each piece into strips; blue strips should measure 2 × 20 inches; white strips should measure 3¼ × 20 inches; and red strips should measure ¾ × 20 inches. Take one strip of each color and line them up along one long edge. Sew along this edge to create an overlapping red, white, and blue ribbon. Repeat this process with all the strips.

3 Take one ribbon and fold it several times to make a concertina. Push a needle and thread through the concertina along the sewn line where the fabric is joined. To make your round rosette shape, pull

tight on the thread and bend the two sides of the concertina around to meet each other, adding a stitch to secure. Do this with all the ribbons.

4 Now add your photos. First, cut out circles from your gold card stock—you need enough to stick onto all your rosettes. Use something round of the correct size as a template (try the bottom of a glass). Select the images you like (you'll find a wide selection online), resize them to fit within the gold circles, and print them out. Cut out these images in circles slightly smaller than your gold circles. Stick one image to each of the gold circles, using the glue stick. Then use your glue gun to stick one image in the center of each of your rosettes.

5 Now all the rosettes are complete, simply attach them to the rope or cord at regular intervals, using a couple of hand-sewn stitches.

How to Create a
VARIETY of VICTORY ROLLS

The VE Day Victory Roll hairstyle is perhaps the most famous and well-known vintage do of them all. The most important advice for those attempting this look is to tease, tease, tease! Don't be afraid, because the hair gets smoothed out when you brush it through with a good-quality bristle brush. The teasing gives the hair volume and texture, and it helps you control where you place your rolls to give the style good structure.

YOU WILL NEED

 hair mousse tail comb curling tongs curl clips section clips

 bristle brush hairspray bobby pins and hairpins

◁ **STEP 1** Create a side parting. Curl and set your hair (*see* page 100) into three curls at the front, on one side of the parting. Use section clips to section off the hair from your crown to the front of your ear on both sides of the parting. The back of the hair can be styled in any way you like; curled, straight, or pinned up in a neat chignon. We went for a soft "pageboy" curl. To achieve this look, section and curl the hair at the back, using curling tongs, and, while each curl is still hot, roll the hair under and pin it into place with a curl clip. Let these curls cool.

▷ **STEP 2** Take out the back curls once they have cooled, leaving the front three curls secured for the moment. Using the bristle brush, gently brush out the curls while using your hands to encourage the hair curl under.

STREET TEA PARTY

220

◁ **STEP 3** Now, using both hands, roll the teased side section of hair toward your parting and secure it with bobby pins. Use hairpins to close up any gaps at the back of the roll—you don't want victory rolls that you can see straight through, like a telescope!

▷ **STEP 4** Repeat steps 2 and 3 on the other side. You can play around with symmetrical or asymmetrical rolls, whatever look best suits you.

◁ **STEP 5** Finally, take the front three curls out of clips and, using your fingers, style this section of hair into a curl with a dramatic wave. Secure it in place with hairpins and bobby pins.

PICNIC TEA PARTY

The British Summer Picnic is a rarity for most by
default. With unpredictable weather and busy lives, the
planets really do need to align for everyone to be available when
the sun has put his hat on (hip, hip hoorah) and is coming out to play.
The unspoken rules of the picnic are such that everyone brings a little
something with them. The list of necessities—food, drink, rugs, games,
and, of course, kitchen paraphernalia—is a lot for one person alone.
This chapter celebrates the great outdoors, with recipes that make the
most not only of what's in season but also of dishes that can cope with
being transported from the kitchen to the picnic rug
and still look delectable.

Fancy a Picnic?

FANCY a LaBeL?

Although the quiche is a French dish, us Brits have been making savory custard cooked in pastry shells since the fourteenth century. I don't think I've ever been to a picnic where someone has not brought a quiche with them, probably simply because they are so easy to make, taste great cold, and travel well!

Pea & Salmon Quiche

SERVES 6

PREP 15 mins, plus freezing and standing

COOK 50–60 mins

1 store-bought rolled dough pie crust, thawed if frozen

all-purpose flour, for dusting

10 ounces cooked salmon fillet, bones and skin removed, flaked

½ cup frozen peas

1 teaspoon finely grated lemon rind

1 teaspoon chopped dill

salt and black pepper

3 eggs

1 cup heavy cream

pinch of ground nutmeg

1 Preheat the oven to 400°F. Put a baking sheet in the oven. Roll out the pie dough on a lightly floured work surface and use it to line the bottom and sides of a 9-inch diameter, loose-bottom fluted tart pan, trimming it to fit. Prick the bottom with a fork. Freeze for 15 minutes or until firm, then place the tart pan on the hot baking sheet in the oven. Bake for 10–15 minutes or until golden. Remove the tart pan from the oven and reduce the oven temperature to 350°F.

2 Combine the salmon, peas, lemon rind, and dill in a bowl and season. Arrange the mixture inside the cooked pastry shell.

3 Beat the eggs, then add the cream, combining well. Pour this over the salmon mixture in the pastry shell. Bake for 40–45 minutes or until golden and just set. Let the quiche stand for at least 5 minutes before serving.

The picnic is a part of British history that has inspired many cultural interpretations: think *The Wind in the Willows* (Ratty and Mole at the boating picnic), or Jane Austen's *Emma* (the ill-fated trip to Box Hill). It would, therefore, be a crime to leave out the British Scone (like an American biscuit) on such a sunny day. You may opt for the classic sweet variety, but this savory version is a great take on the ever-popular cheese sandwich!

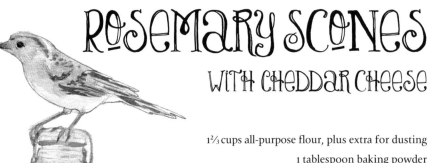

ROSEMARY SCONES
WITH CHEDDAR CHEESE

MAKES 6

PREP 15 mins

COOK 12–15 mins

1⅔ cups all-purpose flour, plus extra for dusting

1 tablespoon baking powder

6 tablespoons butter, plus extra for serving

good pinch of salt

1 teaspoon sweet paprika

½ teaspoon English mustard powder

1 tablespoon chopped rosemary

½ cup cold milk, plus extra, if needed, and for glazing

To serve

Cheddar cheese

chutney

1 Preheat the oven to 400°F. Line a baking sheet with nonstick parchment paper. Sift the flour and baking powder into a bowl. Add the butter and cut it into the flour with a butter knife. With your fingertips, rub it in until the mixture resembles fine bread crumbs. Add the salt, paprika, mustard powder, and rosemary and combine well.

2 Add the milk and stir, first with the butter knife, then with your hands, until just mixed. Add extra milk if there are dry parts.

3 Place the dough on a lightly floured work surface and pat it down to about ½–¾ inch thick. Cut it into 2-inch circles using a pastry cutter.

4 Brush some milk onto the tops of your scones, then bake for 12–15 minutes. Serve with butter, cheddar cheese, and chutney.

What makes this pie a picnic pie? "The vegetable decoration!" I hear you cry. Well, kind of. It's not just the delicious pastry and robust fillings—their freezability also earns them the title of "picnic pie" (honestly, no one will know), so you get to spend less time in the kitchen. It's hard looking fabulous and making delicious food. I need every bit of help I can get!

PICNIC PIES

MAKES 6

PREP 45 mins, plus cooling and resting

COOK 1 hour

1 Heat the olive oil in a large saucepan set over low–medium heat. Cook the onion and carrot for 5–7 minutes. Increase the heat and add the chicken, sweet potatoes, mushrooms, and soup. When the mixture comes to a boil, reduce the heat to a simmer and check the consistency. If it is too watery, add the cornstarch mixed with 1 tablespoon cold water, stirring all the time. Season, then cook for a few more minutes until the mixture thickens. Remove from the heat and set aside to cool completely.

2 Preheat the oven to 350°F. Lightly grease a 6-cup muffin pan (each cup should have a diameter of 3 inches and a depth of 1¼ inches) with lard or vegetable shortening.

3 For the pastry dough, sift the flour, salt, and nutmeg into a warmed bowl. Heat the lard with the milk and ⅓ cup water in a small saucepan set over low heat until the fat has melted, then bring to a boil.

4 Make a well in the flour and drop in an egg yolk. Cover the yolk with a little of the flour, then quickly add the hot liquid mixture, stirring with a wooden spoon until mixed and cool enough to handle.

5 Turn out the dough onto a lightly floured board and knead it until it becomes soft and pliable. Shape the dough into a ball, put it on a warm plate, and cover with an inverted bowl. Let it stand in a warm place to rest for about 20 minutes.

6 Take two-thirds of the dough and cut this into six equal parts. (Keep the other third warm while making the pastry shells.) Roll each of these into a ball and put one into each of the cups in the pan. Using your thumb, quickly press each ball flat onto the bottom, then up the sides to the top edge. Press the dough over the rim of the top edge; it should overlap by at least ¼ inch.

7 Divide the filling into six equal parts, then spoon these into the pie shells.

8 Roll out the remaining dough and cut out six circles using a 3¼-inch pastry cutter. Using a fork, lightly beat the remaining egg yolk in a small bowl. Then, using a pastry brush, paint some of the egg yolk around the upper edges of the pastry and gently press on the lids. Use a small fork to press the rim of each lid against the top of the pie shell, make a hole in the top of each pie, then glaze with the remaining yolk. Bake the pies for 40 minutes on the middle shelf of the oven. Let them cool on a wire rack.

1 tablespoon olive oil

1 small onion, chopped

1 carrot, chopped

10 ounces skinless chicken meat, deboned and cubed

1 small sweet potato, peeled and chopped

1½ cups halved baby cremini mushrooms

1 (14-ounce) can chicken and mushroom soup

1 tablespoon cornstarch (optional)

salt and black pepper

6 baby carrots with tops, to decorate

For the pastry dough

2¾ cups all-purpose flour, plus extra for dusting

½ teaspoon salt

good grating of nutmeg

½ lard or vegetable shortening, plus extra for greasing

⅓ cup milk

2 extra-large egg yolks

9 When cold, store the pies in an airtight container in the refrigerator; they'll keep like this for a couple of days, but bring them to room temperature before eating and garnish by sticking a little baby carrot into the hole of each pie.

Orange and fennel is an uplifting combination. The citrus from the orange and the anise from the fennel are so harmonious, you would think they had been playing croquet together all their lives! This is a dish I always offer to make for a picnic, because it's so quick and yummy. I transport the salads in old jars, often one per person and, depending on how much time I have, I even garnish them!

A summer picnic would not be complete without melon. My mom used watermelon for pacifiers, and would sit my brother and I down in front of a plate of melon slices for hours. We would demolish a whole watermelon between us. This gelatin offers a far more elegant, grown-up way of eating melon; it screams out summer and it looks stunning served in old teacups.

ORANGE & FENNEL PICNIC JARS

½ teaspoon salt

3 oranges, peeled and thinly sliced

1 tablespoon olive oil

1 large fennel bulb

½ red onion, thinly sliced

black pepper

1 teaspoon balsamic vinegar

MAKES 4

PREP 15 mins

1 Sprinkle the salt over the orange slices and drizzle with the olive oil. Put these aside while you are preparing the fennel to let the salt bring out the citrus juices.

2 Quarter the fennel bulb, then thinly slice it, reserving some of the fronds for garnishing. Toss the fennel slices with the orange and red onion slices and season the mixture with black pepper.

3 Drizzle the salad with the balsamic vinegar and toss it again. Divide the salad among four jars, sprinkle with some snipped fennel fronds to garnish, then secure the lids ready for your picnic.

WATERMELON & CANTALOUPE GELATIN

½ cantaloupe (about 3½ pounds), halved and seeded

1 wedge of seedless watermelon (about 2¼ pounds)

3½ tablespoons plain powdered gelatin

3 cups apple juice

¼ cup honey

2 tablespoons small mint leaves

SERVES 6

PREP 15 mins, plus cooling and chilling

COOK 5 mins

1 Scoop out the cantaloupe and watermelon with a melon baller, divide the balls among six teacups (or ramekins, for picnic portability), and set aside.

2 In a medium saucepan, cover the gelatin with the apple juice and 1 cup water and let stand for 5 minutes. Set the pan over low heat, letting the gelatin dissolve; do not let it boil. Turn off the heat and stir in the honey until dissolved, then stir in mint leaves. Let the mixture cool to room temperature, then pour the cooled liquid over the melon and place the teacups or ramekins in the refrigerator for about 3 hours, until set.

After this picnic chapter, you will have no fear about making pastry in your sleep! These sweet Butter & Walnut Tarts are mouthfuls of nutty heaven. Making this recipe is basically a show-off way of bringing the nuts along.

BUTTER & WALNUT TARTS

MAKES 6

PREP 15 mins, plus chilling

COOK 18–20 mins

For the pastry dough

1²⁄₃ cups all-purpose flour, plus extra for dusting

½ cup unsweetened cocoa powder

⅓ cup confectioners' sugar

pinch of salt

1¼ sticks butter, chilled and cubed, plus extra for greasing

3 egg yolks

For the filling

6 tablespoons butter, softened

½ cup firmly packed light brown sugar

1 teaspoon vanilla extract

1 extra-large egg, beaten

½ cup liquid glucose

½ cup finely chopped walnuts

1 Preheat the oven to 375°F. Grease a flexible 6-cup muffin pan or a standard 6-cup muffin pan lined with foil tart liners.

2 To make the pastry dough, combine the flour with the cocoa powder, confectioners' sugar, and salt in a food processor. Blend in the butter until the mixture resembles coarse bread crumbs. Mix in the eggs and blend to form a ball. Wrap the dough tightly in plastic wrap and chill in the refrigerator for 30 minutes.

3 Roll out the dough on a lightly floured work surface into a thin sheet. Stamp out six 4-inch circles with a pastry cutter and use these to line the muffin cups or foil tart liners.

4 For the filling, cream the butter with the sugar and vanilla extract. Beat in the egg and the liquid glucose. Spoon the nuts into the prepared pastry shells. Divide the rest of the filling among the pastry shells; be sure none is more than two-thirds full.

5 Bake the tarts for 18–20 minutes, or until the filling is golden and bubbly.

A cobbler is halfway between a fruit crisp and a pie. I love it because you can use your sweet juicy homegrown fruit for the filling, which can sometimes be sharp but, topped with a sweet crunchy cobbler, it is summer lovin' in a clip-top jar.

RHUbaRb Cobbler
in a Jar

SERVES 6

PREP 20 mins, plus cooling

COOK 20 mins

For the filling

5 stalks rhubarb, trimmed and chopped into ½-inch pieces

½ cup superfine sugar or granulated sugar, plus extra for sprinkling

½ vanilla bean

grated rind and juice of ½ orange

For the cobbler

¾ cup all-purpose flour

2 tablespoons cornmeal

¼ cup granulated sugar

¼ teaspoon baking soda

¾ teaspoon baking powder

¼ teaspoon salt

5 tablespoons butter, melted

⅓ cup buttermilk

½ teaspoon vanilla extract

1 Preheat the oven to 350°F.

2 For the filling, place the rhubarb in a large bowl with the sugar. Split open the vanilla bean and scrape out the seeds into the bowl. Add the orange rind and juice. Mix well and divide the mixture evenly among six clip-top jars.

3 To make the cobbler, combine the flour, cornmeal, sugar, baking soda, baking powder, and salt in a large bowl. In a small bowl, beat together the melted butter, buttermilk, and vanilla extract. Add the wet ingredients to the dry ingredients and stir to combine with a rubber spatula.

4 To assemble the cobbler, divide the dough into six equal pieces and place each in a jar on top of the rhubarb mixture. Sprinkle each mound of dough with some sugar. Place the jars in a baking pan and add hot water to the pan until it reaches halfway up the outsides of the jars. Bake for about 20 minutes, until the filling is bubbling and the cobblers are golden brown on top and cooked through. Cool on a wire rack for 20 minutes before serving or, if you're planning to take them somewhere, let them cool until just kind of warm before putting on the lids.

When plums arrive, the vacation season starts. The decadent sweet almond frangipane and the fruity plum in this dish could be considered a twist on the classic British "Bakewell" tart. This dessert is on my list of all-time favorites and works well with cherries, pears, peaches, apples, and berries—in fact, every type of fruit. Don't be frugal with the frangipane; you want people to close their eyes in delight when eating these!

PREP 20 mins, plus chilling

BAKE 30–40 mins

MAKES 6

Frangipane & Plum Tarts

For the pastry dough

1²⁄₃ cups all-purpose flour, plus extra for dusting

2 tablespoons superfine sugar or granulated sugar

7 tablespoons butter, chilled and cubed, plus extra for greasing

1 egg

For the frangipane

3½ tablespoons unsalted butter, softened

¼ cup firmly packed light brown sugar

½ egg

½ cup ground almonds (almond meal)

½ teaspoon almond extract

For the tart filling

3 ripe plums, pitted and cut into ½-inch slices

1 To make the pastry dough, sift the flour into a large bowl and add the sugar and cubed butter, then rub between your fingertips until the mixture resembles fine bread crumbs.

2 In a small bowl, beat the egg with 2 tablespoons iced water. Pour this into the flour mixture and slowly bring the ingredients together with your hands to form a dough, being careful not to overwork it. Add extra iced water, if required.

3 Knead the dough gently on a lightly floured work surface, then wrap it in plastic wrap and chill in the refrigerator for at least 30 minutes, until firm.

4 To make the frangipane, cream the butter and sugar together with a wooden spoon or an electric mixer until light and fluffy. Stir in the egg. Add the ground almonds and almond extract and mix well until everything is combined. Set aside.

5 Preheat the oven to 350°F. Roll out the dough thinly on a lightly floured work surface. Use the dough to line six individual tart pans that are 3¼ inches in diameter. Trim away any excess. Line each pan with nonstick parchment paper and fill it with pie weights or dried beans. Put the pans on a baking sheet and bake for 12 minutes. Remove the paper and weights and bake for another 5 minutes. Let cool.

6 Spoon the frangipane into the tart shells so that it reaches about halfway up the sides. Smooth over the surfaces with a spatula and cover the frangipane evenly with the plum slices.

7 Bake the tarts for 15–20 minutes or until the pastry is crisp and golden brown and the fruit is tender. Remove the tarts from the oven and serve immediately, or let cool and serve at room temperature.

THE COMMON TIGER

This ambrosial drink makes you feel like you are swallowing summer. It's light, sweet, and calming. It also works very well with a dash of vodka, for an adult kick!

CHAMOMILE COOLER

SERVES 6

PREP
10 mins,
plus steeping
and cooling

2½ cups dried chamomile flowers

2 tablespoons dried lemon verbena leaves

¼ cup honey

ice cubes

1 In a large saucepan set over high heat, bring 5 cups water to a boil. Take the pan off the heat and stir in the chamomile flowers and lemon verbena leaves. Cover the pan and let the mixture steep for 10 minutes.

2 Meanwhile, place a large strainer lined with cheesecloth or damp paper towels over another saucepan or heatproof bowl. Strain the tea through the cheesecloth, pressing on the herbs with the back of a wooden spoon to extract all the liquid.

3 Stir in the honey until it dissolves, then leave the tea for about 1 hour to cool completely. Fill six tall glasses with ice cubes, pour the tea over the ice, and serve immediately.

I'm not a lover of anything beer-flavored, but give me sunshine and the flavor of lemons and my taste buds must change! This shandy has a Mexican twist; it's almost a beer cocktail! Old glass bottles with narrow necks make great glasses and stop the insects from getting drunk!

SUMMER SHANDY

¼ cup sea salt

juice of 6 limes, squeezed lime shells reserved

crushed ice

8½ cups Mexican beer, such as Corona

½ cup lemon-flavored soda

Tabasco or Worcestershire sauce, to serve (optional)

SERVES 6

PREP
10 mins

1 Pour the salt onto a plate. Wipe the tops of six glass bottles (each with a minimum capacity of 1½ cups) with the lime shells, then dip them into the salt to leave a salt rim.

2 Put some crushed ice into a large pitcher, then add the lime juice and beer. Finish with a dash of lemon-flavored soda and a few drops of Tabasco or Worcestershire sauce, if you like. Pour the drink through a funnel into the bottles.

How to Make a
Head Scarf Blanket

Good ideas are born out of need. I've always wanted a stylish picnic blanket, but never found one. Gingham just does not float my boat. What does, however, are the bright and energetic head scarves that I continually pick up for next to nothing! Can you see where I'm going with this?

YOU WILL NEED

✂ heavyweight iron-on interfacing (enough to cover the wrong side of each scarf)

✂ 4 square head scarves of the same size that work together as a set ✂ iron

✂ fabric scissors ✂ sewing machine ✂ thread to match scarves and binding

✂ calico (enough to cover the same area as all 4 scarves when sewn together) ✂ pins

✂ bias binding tape (enough to bind the edges of all 4 scarves when sewn together,

so measure 1 edge of a scarf and multiply by 8)

1 First, iron a sheet of interfacing onto the wrong sides of each of your head scarves, then cut around the edges.

2 Take two scarves and lay them on top of one another, right sides together. Sew along one side to join. Repeat this with the other two scarves. You should now have two sets of two scarves sewn together. You now need to use the same technique to join these pieces to make a square, so that all four pieces are joined together like patchwork.

3 Cut out a piece of calico the same size as your patchwork square. Lay your patchwork on top of the calico, right sides facing out, and pin into place. Now sew all the way around the edge, using the edge of the pressure foot as a guide to the seam allowance, joining the calico to the back of your patchwork. (Make sure your fabrics are ironed flat before you start sewing.)

4 Now to finish the edges. Take the end of your binding and fold the tape in half around the edge of your blanket at a corner. Begin slowly sewing it in place, folding and positioning it as you work. When you get to another corner, go very slowly around it and ease the tape around the corner. When you have gone all the way around, cut off the excess tape and tidy the rough ends of the tape by turning them under and finishing with a couple of hand stitches.

HOW TO CREATE THE CAT EARS TURBAN

If you want an authentically vintage but fuss-free hairdo for your picnic tea party, look no farther than the turban. Known by the French as *Cache Misère* (which means to "camouflage misery"), the turban is perfect for unpredictable weather and, of course, bad hair days! This way of wearing the turban is from the 1940s and looks just as stylish now as it did then.

YOU WILL NEED

✂ long scarf ✂ bobby pins

▷ **STEP 1** Fold your scarf in half into a triangle, then wrap it around your head. Tightly knot it at the front of your head. Tuck the triangle at the end of the scarf under the knot.

◁ **STEP 2** Take one of the ends of the scarf and roll it inward toward the knot.

◁ **STEP 3** Tuck this end into the turban at the front edge, shaping it to form a "cat's ear." Repeat on the other side. Secure the scarf in place with a bobby pin and smile!

FIREWORKS TEA PARTY

Remember, remember the 5th of November?
I certainly do.

I remember my mom shouting at me to stay away from the fireworks and bonfire and to be careful of the sparklers. And I remember the FOOD. Food that warms the heart—sausages, soup, pie, caramel apples, marshmallows, hot chocolate, and warm cider.

In my teenage years, I began to understand the history behind the celebration, when Guy Fawkes failed to blow up the House of Lords in 1605, which is now celebrated in England every 5th of November as Guy Fawkes Night (or Bonfire Night). I couldn't wait for it to arrive so that I could write my name in the air with my sparkler and eat all this delicious food!

It's safe to say that the sausage sandwich is a Bonfire Night staple. Easy to make and juicy to eat, it checks all the right boxes. But for the exhibitionist in you, this just might not be elaborate enough (gosh, I wish I was not such a show-off). Be generous with the filling when you prepare this dish—the juicy sausage and onions need to be the star!

Sausage & Onion cups

For the bread

3⅓ cups white bread flour, plus extra for dusting

2 teaspoons active dry yeast

2 teaspoons granulated sugar

1½ teaspoons salt

1 tablespoon butter, plus extra for greasing

milk, for glazing

1 tablespoon sesame seeds, for sprinkling

vegetable oil, for oiling

For the filling

1 tablespoon butter

1 onion, halved and thinly sliced

½ teaspoon granulated sugar

12 Vienna or small sausages

MAKES 6

PREP 35–40 mins, plus proving

COOK 35 mins

1 Grease six small ceramic sugar bowls or teacups on the inside with some butter.

2 For the filling, melt the butter in a large, deep skillet set over a low heat and add the onion. Cover and cook gently for about 10 minutes, until the onion has softened. Remove the lid, add the sugar, then cook for another 10 minutes, stirring, until all of the liquid has evaporated and the onion has turned golden.

3 To make the bread, place the flour, yeast, sugar, and salt in a large bowl and rub in the butter with your fingertips. Add 1 cup lukewarm water and mix to a soft dough.

4 Turn out the dough on a lightly floured work surface and knead it by folding it toward you, then pushing down and away from you with the heel of your hand. Give the dough a quarter turn and repeat the action. Knead for about 10–15 minutes, until it is smooth, elastic, and no longer sticky.

5 Place the dough in a bowl and cover with plastic wrap. Let sit somewhere warm for 1–1½ hours or until doubled in size. Then remove it from the bowl and gently punch the air out of it. Cut it into even pieces and place a piece in each of the prepared bowls or teacups, which should be placed on a baking sheet. Glaze with milk and sprinkle with the sesame seeds.

6 Place the baking sheet of bowls or cups inside a large oiled plastic bag and let sit in a warm place to rise for about 45–60 minutes. The dough is ready if, when prodded on the side, the indentation remains.

7 Preheat the oven to 425°F. Gently pry a hole in the middle of each ball of dough and fill it with two sausages and some onion mixture.

8 Bake on the middle shelf of the oven for about 15 minutes, depending on the size of your bowls or teacups, or until the bread is browned and sounds hollow when tapped.

Soup is a friend on any cold day and is perfect to warm your heart and your hands! With pumpkins lining every street around this time of the year, it would be crazy not to celebrate this winter vegetable, which is complemented perfectly by some spice. This soup is best made the day before, giving you more time to get ready and position your winter beret on Guy Fawkes Night.

SPICY PUMPKIN SOUP

SERVES 6
PREP 15 mins
COOK 35–40 mins

1 tablespoon vegetable oil

1 red onion, chopped

2 garlic cloves, crushed

½ teaspoon ground coriander

½ teaspoon ground cumin

½ teaspoon chili powder, or to taste

2¼ pounds of pumpkin, peeled, seeded, and chopped into medium pieces

4 cups chicken or vegetable stock

⅓ cup heavy cream

black pepper

To serve

crème fraîche or sour cream

chopped chives

Rustic Bonfire Bread (*see page 254*)

1 Heat the oil in a saucepan and cook the onion over medium heat for 3–4 minutes. Add the garlic and spices and cook for another 1 minute.

2 Add the pumpkin and stock to the saucepan, bring to a boil, then simmer for 20–30 minutes or until the pumpkin is tender. Remove the pan from the heat and set it aside to let the contents cool slightly.

3 Process the pumpkin and the cooking liquid, in batches, in a food processor or blender until smooth.

4 Return the soup to a clean saucepan, stir in the cream, season to taste with black pepper, and cook over medium heat, without boiling, until heated.

5 Serve with a swirl of crème fraîche or sour cream, a sprinkling of chives, and Rustic Bonfire Bread.

My Bonfire-Night secret weapon is this quick bread. Think of it as a bread cake. Mix the ingredients together with a delicate touch, then watch it turn into something delicious in the oven! It happens to taste sublime with Spicy Pumpkin Soup (*see page 252*), or maybe you'd like to use it to make sausage sandwiches, or you could simply eat it toasted with butter.

RUSTIC BONFIRE BREAD

MAKES 8 rolls

PREP 20 mins

COOK 40 mins

1 teaspoon olive oil

1 red onion, finely chopped

1¼ cups whole-wheat flour

½ cup rolled oats

1⅔ cups all-purpose white flour, plus extra for dusting

2 teaspoons cream of tartar

1 teaspoon baking soda

1 teaspoon salt

1 teaspoon granulated sugar

½ teaspoon English mustard powder

2 tablespoons butter, melted

1¼ cups milk, at room temperature

1½ cups shredded sharp cheddar cheese

leaves from 1 sprig of rosemary, chopped

leaves from 1 sprig of thyme

1½ cups chopped sun-dried tomatoes

1 Heat the oil in a skillet, add the onion, and sauté over low heat for 7–10 minutes, until softened. Remove the skillet from the heat and set aside.

2 Heat the oven to 375°F. Sift the dry ingredients into a large bowl and make a large well in the center. Combine the melted butter and milk, then pour the mixture into the well. Mix to a soft dough.

3 Add most of the cheddar, the herbs, onion, and the tomatoes to the dough, then gently knead on a lightly floured work surface to combine. Divide the dough into eight lumps of equal size and shape them into rough circles that are two fingers'-width deep.

4 Place the pieces of dough side by side on a floured baking sheet, sprinkle the remaining cheddar over the top, then bake for 30 minutes, until the rolls are golden brown and the cheese is bubbling. Cool on a wire rack and eat while warm.

This dish is my personal favorite winter warmer. I love the gentle flavors of the sweet leek, the delicateness of the haddock, and the richness that the cream brings, all topped with mouthfuls of silky cheesy mashed potatoes. It can't help but make people smile.

HADDOCK & LEEK PIE
WITH CHEESY MASHED POTATO TOPPING

SERVES 6

PREP 25 mins

COOK 1 hour

6 haddock fillets, about 4 ounces each, or other white fish fillets

2½ cups whole milk

1 bay leaf (optional)

4 tablespoons butter

2 leeks, trimmed, cleaned, and sliced

⅓ cup plus 1 tablespoon all-purpose flour

salt and black pepper

For the cheesy mashed potato topping

4 large russet or Yukon gold potatoes, peeled and cut into quarters

1 tablespoon butter

½ cup milk

salt and black pepper

1 cup shredded Cheddar cheese

1 Place the haddock fillets in a large saucepan set over low-medium heat, cover with the milk, and add the bay leaf, if using. Let the milk slowly come to a boil, then turn off the heat. Place a lid on the pan and let the fish sit in the hot milk for about 7 minutes. Remove the fish and flake it. Reserve the milk for later, removing the bay leaf, if using, at this stage.

2 Meanwhile, make the cheesy mashed potato topping. Boil the potatoes until tender, then drain. Add the butter and milk and mash with a potato masher. Season to taste. Add the cheddar and gently mix in.

3 Preheat the oven to 400°F.

4 Heat the butter in a saucepan set over medium heat. Add the leeks and sauté for 5–6 minutes, until soft. Add the flour, stir well, and cook for another 1–2 minutes. Remove the pan from the heat and gradually stir in the milk that was used to poach the fish. Return the pan to the heat, gently bring up to a simmer, stirring well, and cook for about 5 minutes, until the sauce has thickened. Season with salt and black pepper.

5 Place half the sauce in individual heatproof bowls. Put the haddock fillets on top of the sauce, then spoon the remainder over the fish. Top each bowl with cheesy mashed potatoes. Place the bowls on a baking sheet and bake for 25–30 minutes, until the topping is golden brown.

Eton Mess is a British tradition. I love telling the story of how the students of Eton dropped a meringue to create a mess and the name of this famous dessert was born. It is normally made with fresh berries to break up the sweetness of the cream and meringue. But when it's cold and wintery, if you're like me, you'll want something scrumptiously sweet inside you, and on these occasions, this is your Mr. Perfect—Dr. Banana Eton Mess.

BANANA ETON MESS
WITH CARAMEL BANANA SAUCE

SERVES 6

PREP 25 mins, plus cooling

COOK 7 mins

⅔ cup heavy cream

⅔ cup crème fraîche (or ⅓ cup sour cream mixed with ⅓ cup heavy cream)

3 small store-bought meringues

For the caramel banana sauce

1 stick unsalted butter

½ cup packed dark brown sugar

3 bananas, sliced

½ cup heavy cream

1 tablespoon dark rum

To decorate

1 banana, sliced

chopped mixed nuts (optional)

1 For the sauce, place the butter and sugar in a saucepan and cook over medium heat, stirring continuously, until the mixture darkens and caramelizes. Add the bananas, rum, and the ½ cup heavy cream and stir for a few minutes until the bananas have softened. Let cool.

2 In a separate bowl, beath the ⅔ cup heavy cream together with the crème fraîche until soft peaks form.

3 Break up the meringues using a rolling pin. Stir most of the broken meringues into the cream mixture, reserving a little for decorating.

4 To serve, spoon the meringue-cream mixture into the bottom of six decorative glasses. Add a layer of the caramel banana sauce. Repeat the process with the remaining ingredients, reserving some of the banana sauce to top. Decorate each Eton Mess with banana slices, a sprinkling of chopped nuts, if using, and the remaining meringue and sauce.

In 1908, William W. Kolb invented the toffee apple. This humble candy maker was experimenting with red candy and apples during the festivities and wake of the annual apple harvest season, and the rest, as they say, is sweet history. Don't just stop at these colors; try blue, pink, orange, and even purple. You're getting the gist.

Toffee Blackballs

MAKES 6

PREP 15 mins,
plus cooling

COOK 30 mins

6 unwaxed apples

6 wooden twigs or sticks, trimmed and sprayed with gold or silver edible luster (available online)

1¼ cups granulated sugar

½ teaspoon white wine vinegar

few drops of blackberry-flavored oil (available online)

¼ teaspoon red food coloring

¼ teaspoon black food coloring

1 Cover a baking sheet with a large sheet of nonstick parchment paper.

2 Remove the stems and any leaves from the apples. Make a little hole in the bottom of each apple for the twigs or sticks. Set aside.

3 Combine ½ cup water with the sugar and vinegar in a small, heavy saucepan set over medium heat. Slowly dissolve the sugar, then bring the mixture to a boil.

4 Heat the mixture to 300°F on a candy thermometer. (If you don't have a candy thermometer, test the mixture after 20 minutes of cooking by dropping a spoonful into a cup of cold water. The mixture should become hard and will crack when you tap it with the back of a metal spoon.)

5 Remove the syrup from the heat and, when the mixture has stopped bubbling, stir into it the flavored oil and red food coloring. Let it sit for a little while to thicken up a touch. Dip three apples, one by one, into the syrup, swirling them around to be sure they are evenly coated.

6 Remove each apple from the syrup with a slotted spoon and hold it above the pan to drain off the excess syrup. Place them on the prepared baking sheet, stick a twig or stick into the hole in each apple, and let sit for about 20 minutes to cool and harden.

7 After you've done three apples, add the black coloring to the syrup, then repeat the dipping process. If your syrup thickens or cools too much, simply reheat it briefly before proceeding. Let the apples cool completely before serving.

Bonfire Night was special in my house. The men would bond over failing to light the fireworks, while the women would bond in the kitchen over sweet treats my mom's girlfriends had brought. I don't remember a 5th of November with no ginger cake, chocolate brownies, or marshmallows to toast. Here are my sweet twists that meld together all I remember.

Oatmeal Ginger
Cakes with Brandy Cream

¾ cup all-purpose flour

¾ teaspoon baking powder

1 teaspoon ground ginger

good pinch of allspice

pinch of salt

⅓ cup rolled oats

¾ cup firmly packed dark brown sugar

1 stick butter

⅓ cup light corn syrup

3 tablespoons molasses

1 tablespoon milk

1 extra-large egg

4 pieces preserved ginger in syrup, chopped

For the brandy cream

½ cup heavy whipping cream

1 tablespoon confectioners' sugar

2 tablespoons brandy

MAKES 6

PREP 15 mins, plus cooling

COOK 25–30 mins

1 Preheat the oven to 350°F. Sift the flour, baking powder, spices, and salt into a bowl. Stir in the oats and sugar and make a well in the center.

2 Meanwhile, melt the butter, corn syrup, and molasses gently, whisking to emulsify, then remove from the heat and let cool a little. Mix this into the flour mixture with a wooden spoon. Beat the milk and egg together and mix into the mixture. Fold in the ginger.

3 Pour the batter into six deep, individual molds and bake for 20–25 minutes, until the batter is still slightly soft to the touch. Let cool for 30 minutes before turning out.

4 For the brandy cream, whip the cream and sugar together until soft peaks form, then fold in the brandy.

Guy "Forks" Marshmallow Brownies

8 ounces semisweet chocolate

2¼ sticks butter, cubed

1¼ cups firmly packed dark brown sugar

4 eggs

1½ cups all-purpose flour, sifted

⅓ cup cocoa powder, sifted

¼ teaspoon baking powder

2 teaspoons ground cinnamon

22 marshmallows (about 5½ ounces), chopped

MAKES 16

PREP 10 mins

COOK 55 mins– 1 hour 5 mins

1 Preheat the oven to 325°F. Then line an 8-inch square cake pan with nonstick parchment paper.

2 Break the chocolate into pieces and melt it with the butter in a heatproof bowl set over a saucepan of barely simmering water; do not let the bottom of the bowl touch the water below. Let cool slightly.

3 Place the sugar, eggs, flour, cocoa powder, baking powder, and cinnamon in a bowl. Add the chocolate mixture and mix until combined. Fold in the marshmallows and pour the batter into the prepared baking pan. Bake for 50–60 minutes or until a toothpick inserted into the center of the cake comes out clean. Let cool slightly in the pan before slicing into 16 bite-size pieces. Pierce a small fork into the top of half of the bites and arrange them in a checkerboard fashion.

If you are all to brave the great outdoors on Bonfire Night, the drinks you intend to serve to your friends must be warm. Hot chocolate is a classic choice but, made with real chocolate, it's a no-brainer for adults (with, maybe, a dash of sweet liqueur) and children alike. Spicy Hot Perry, on the other hand, is lighter and spicier. I wonder what Guy Fawkes was drinking while guarding the gunpowder? Here's to Guy ... for being caught and not blowing up parliament!

DELICIOUS HOT CHOCOLATE

SERVES 6
PREP 5 mins
COOK 5 mins

5 cups milk

1¼ cups heavy cream

8 ounces semisweet chocolate, broken into pieces, plus extra grated, to serve

dash of orange liqueur for each of the grown-ups

1 Place the milk, cream, and chocolate in a saucepan. Bring gently to a boil, whisking until smooth.

2 Serve in six individual cups, adding a dash of orange liqueur and a little grated chocolate to each.

SPICY HOT PERRY

SERVES 6
PREP 2 mins, plus steeping
COOK 10 mins

5 cups perry (hard pear cider), pear juice, or apple juice

1 tablespoon packed dark brown sugar

2 cinnamon sticks, plus extra to decorate

4 cloves

4 black peppercorns

4 allspice berries

1 Put all the ingredients into a saucepan and simmer over medium heat for 5 minutes. Take the pan off the heat and let the mixture steep for 20 minutes. Reheat, then strain and serve. Decorate each glass with a cinnamon stick.

HOW TO MAKE
BONFIRE MITTENS

What do you do when a well-loved old woollen sweater tragically dies? Felt it to make a cozy pair of stylish bonfire mittens, of course! To felt it, simply wash the sweater on a hot cycle with plenty of detergent and let dry.

1 Use a photocopier to enlarge the mitten template, below, at 400 percent and cut it out. Position the hand template with its straight edge aligned with the ribbed bottom of the felted sweater (to give your mittens a nice ribbed cuff) and pin in place. Position the thumb template on the sweater and pin in place. Cut out the fabric pieces by cutting around the templates. Flip the templates, pin in place, and repeat to cut out felt pieces for the other hand.

2 Fold a thumb piece in half with the right side of the fabric facing inward, so that the corners (shown on the left and right sides of the template) meet. Hand sew from the corners to the top of the thumb (with the two adjacent curves) in blanket stitch or running stitch, working close to the edges of the fabric. Be sure that, when you sew the second thumb, it is the mirror image of the first.

3 Position the left thumb piece on the left-hand piece. It is best to put the

thumb piece on your thumb, put the hand piece on your hand, and push your thumb through the hole in the hand piece to get a good idea of how to position the thumb piece on the hand piece. Sew the thumb piece in place as before, with the right sides of the fabric facing each other. Repeat with the right hand and thumb pieces.

4 Fold each mitten in half and sew along the outer edge to complete the glove. Turn the right sides out, and your mittens are ready to wear!

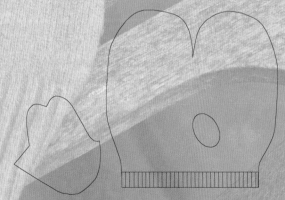

How to Make
Bonfire Night Rockets

Finding quirky Bonfire Night decorations is a challenge. Yes, it's about the fireworks but, let's face it, once your dad or boyfriend lights a few rockets (as long as it's legal in your state), and everyone oohs and ahhs and shouts "be careful," it's all about the food, the decor, and being with good friends! These homemade decorative rockets look great, can be put into any vessel, and take as long to make as it takes my dad to burn the sausages.

YOU WILL NEED

✂ plain paper ✂ access to a computer and printer ✂ paper scissors

✂ several cardboard toilet roll tubes (1 tube per rocket) ✂ glue gun and

glue stick ✂ compass ✂ selection of colored card stock ✂ hack saw

✂ 6½ feet of ⅛-inch-wide wooden dowels

1 To start making your rockets, you will need to find suitable designs to use for the labels. You'll easily find vintage designs by searching online. Once you have found some you like, print out a selection. If they are not the right size, you will need to cut them down—an ordinary cardboard toilet roll tube will need a 3¾ × 6-inch label.

2 Wrap one label around each cardboard tube. Glue it in place with a glue stick.

3 Use a compass to draw circles with a 4-inch diameter (one for each rocket) on the colored card stock. Cut them all out.

4 Take a circle and make a snip from the edge to the center, then pull one newly cut edge across the other to overlap them and form a cone shape. Secure the overlap in place with glue, then repeat with all the circles.

5 Now you need to use the glue gun to stick a cone to the top of each cardboard tube, choosing a color that complements each label.

6 Next, use the hacksaw to cut your dowels into pieces of various lengths. Finally, put a dab of glue on the end of each piece of dowel and attach it to the inside of each cardboard tube, positioning it high enough inside the tube to be sure the glue won't show. Your rockets are now ready to brighten up your yard on Bonfire Night!

HOW TO CREATE
THE FIRECRACKER

When it's cold outside but you still want to channel a chic and stylish look at your Guy Fawkes party, try my version of "hat hair." The Firecracker is a sure-fire way of feeling good with sparkle while being sure you keep warm. Who says you have to choose comfort over style? I've chosen a beret, but this style is adaptable for other headwear choices.

YOU WILL NEED

hair mousse ✎ tail comb ✎ curling tongs ✎ curl clips ✎ bristle brush
✎ beret ✎ hairpins and bobby pins

◁ **STEP 1** Curl and set your hair with curling tongs (*see* page 100), with three vertical curls at the front. You will use these to create a voluminous wave.

◁ **STEP 2** Once the curls have cooled, take out all the clips except the three at the front and lightly brush your hair.

◁ **STEP 3** Add the beret, tilted at an angle and pulled slightly lower on the side of your parting. On this side, form pin curls with the hair that is seen peeking from beneath the hat and use hairpins and bobby pins to secure.

▷ **STEP 4** Leave the curls loose on the other side. If you have longer hair, pin the length underneath while keeping the curls in place at the top, creating a faux bob. Remove the clips from the front three curls and gently brush them out into a soft, sweeping wave. Either leave this loose, or put the ends of it into the fuller curls at the sides.

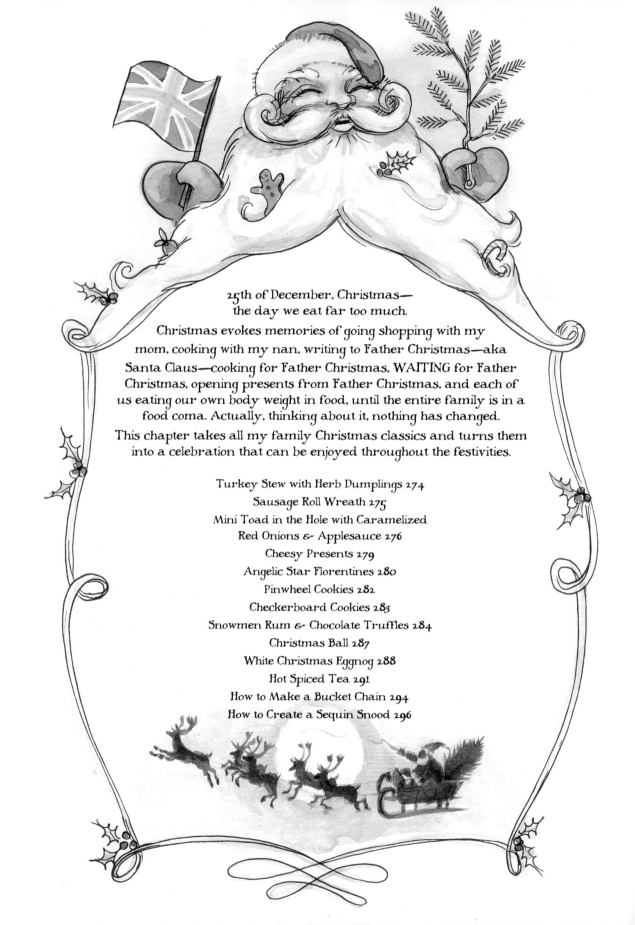

25th of December, Christmas—
the day we eat far too much.

Christmas evokes memories of going shopping with my
mom, cooking with my nan, writing to Father Christmas—aka
Santa Claus—cooking for Father Christmas, WAITING for Father
Christmas, opening presents from Father Christmas, and each of
us eating our own body weight in food, until the entire family is in a
food coma. Actually, thinking about it, nothing has changed.

This chapter takes all my family Christmas classics and turns them
into a celebration that can be enjoyed throughout the festivities.

The turkey took time to be crowned Bird of the British Christmas Table. Peacocks and boars were popular until the turkey graced Henry VIII's Christmas. As an affordable and easily bred bird, turkey won its place by being accessible to the masses. If it's good enough for a king, it's good enough for me, especially in this pie.

TURKEY STEW
WITH HERB DUMPLINGS

SERVES 6
PREP 25 mins
COOK about 1 hour

For the dumplings

1⅓ cups all-purpose flour

½ teaspoon baking powder

¼ teaspoon baking soda

½ teaspoon salt

4 tablespoons butter, cubed

3 tablespoons chopped rosemary, thyme, and parsley (optional)

¾ cup buttermilk

1 extra-large egg

For the filling

4 tablespoons butter

⅓ cup plus 1 tablespoon all-purpose flour

3 cups turkey stock or a combination of stock and leftover gravy

1 teaspoon dried thyme

1 bay leaf

salt and black pepper

½ teaspoon freshly grated nutmeg

¼ teaspoon Worcestershire sauce

1½ pounds cooked turkey or chicken, cut into strips

1⅓ cups frozen peas

1 To make the dumplings, combine the flour, baking powder, baking soda, and salt in a bowl. Add the butter and rub it in with your fingertips until the mixture resembles coarse bread crumbs. Stir in the herbs, if using. Cover and refrigerate this mixture while you're making the filling.

2 Preheat the oven to 400°F.

3 To make the filling, melt the butter over medium heat in a large, shallow flameproof casserole dish or dutch oven with a lid. Whisk in the flour and cook for 3 minutes, stirring occasionally.

4 Take the dish off the heat and add the stock or stock and gravy, 1 cup at a time, whisking it in to prevent lumps from forming. Return the mixture to the heat and season with the thyme, bay leaf, salt and black pepper, nutmeg, and Worcestershire sauce. Simmer the sauce for 15 minutes, then stir in the meat and peas. Return the filling to a simmer.

5 Meanwhile, whisk the buttermilk and egg together and add this to the dry dumpling mixture all at once. Stir together until evenly moistened. This should be a loose mixture.

6 Scoop a tablespoonful of the mixture into a dumpling shape (like a meatball) and place this in the casserole dish with the filling. Repeat with the remaining dumpling mixture—you should have about 12 dumplings. Make sure you leave space between them in the casserole, because they will expand to almost double their size during cooking. Put the lid on the dish and bake for 40–45 minutes.

At Christmas, my mom always put an evergreen wreath on our front door. It always felt inviting and, apparently, it signifies the hope we feel with the oncoming spring and the renewed light. I love this edible take on it, partly because it's delicious, but mostly because everyone oohs at the cuteness factor. I won't tell them it took just 20 minutes to make!

Sausage Roll wreath

SERVES 14

PREP 20 mins, plus chilling

COOK 20—25 mins

1 sheet ready-to-bake puff pastry
14 Vienna or other small sausages
1 egg, beaten

1 Reserving one-fifth of the pastry, roll the remaining pastry into an 8¼ × 9½-inch rectangle. Cut this in half down the middle so that you have two sheets that are 8¼ × 4¾ inches. Now cut these into 14 rectangles that are 1¼ × 4¾ inches.

2 Wrap one strip of dough around each small sausage. Roll the remaining one-fifth dough into a long, thin strip and form a circle on a baking sheet lined with nonstick parchment paper. Brush the circle with some

of the beaten egg and place the mini sausage rolls on top of the pastry circle, side by side, so that each sausage roll is just touching the next.

3 Brush the sausage rolls with the remaining beaten egg, then chill in the refrigerator for 20 minutes.

4 Preheat the oven to 400°F. Remove the baking sheet with the wreath from the refrigerator and bake for 20–25 minutes, until golden brown and puffed up. Serve immediately.

I've often wondered how this delicious combination of batter and sausage got its British name, but the origin is disputed. The tasty sausages nestling in their crunchy homes must be eaten with onions and sweet apple and, if you want to take the seasonal festivities a step farther, add some cinnamon.

Mini TOAD IN THE HOLE
WITH CARAMELIZED RED ONIONS & APPLESAUCE

MAKES 16

PREP 25 mins, plus resting

COOK 1½ hours

For the caramelized red onions

1 tablespoon olive oil

1 red onion, thinly sliced

¼ cup granulated sugar

2 tablespoons red wine vinegar

salt and black pepper

For the batter

⅔ cup all-purpose flour

½ teaspoon baking powder

1 free-range egg

½ cup milk

salt and black pepper

1 teaspoon vegetable oil

16 Vienna or other small sausages

For the applesauce

2 tablespoons butter

1 Pippin apple, peeled, cored, and diced

2 tablespoons granulated sugar

¼ cup apple juice

squeeze of lemon

To garnish

1 teaspoon olive oil

16 sage leaves

1 For the caramelized onions, heat the oil in a saucepan over low heat and soften the onion for about 10 minutes, without letting it color.

2 Stir in the sugar and vinegar. Season and cook gently over low heat for 45 minutes, until the onions turn a lovely dark golden color (if it looks like they might stick to the pan, add a splash of water). Taste and add a little more sugar or vinegar, if needed. Aim for a sweet and tangy flavor. Set aside.

3 To make the batter, sift the flour and baking powder into a large bowl and make a well in the center. Whisk the egg in a small bowl with the milk and add ¼ cup water, stirring to combine. Pour this mixture gradually into the well in the flour, whisking until all the flour has been incorporated. Aim for this mixture to have the consistency of smooth heavy cream—you may not need all the liquid. Season well and let the batter rest for 15 minutes.

4 Preheat the oven to 425°F.

5 Divide the 1 teaspoon vegetable oil evenly among the cups of a 16-cup miniature muffin pan and place in the oven for 5 minutes, until the oil is smoking hot.

6 Place a small sausage in each muffin cup, then divide the batter among the muffin cups. Bake for 20–25 minutes, until the batter has puffed up and is golden.

7 Meanwhile, for the applesauce, heat a large skillet over medium heat and add the butter. When the butter has melted and is starting to foam, add the apple and sugar. Cook over medium heat for 5 minutes or until the edges of the apple pieces start to brown. Add the apple and lemon juices and cook over medium heat until the apples are golden brown and the sauce has thickened.

8 For the garnish, heat the oil in a small skillet. Cook the sage leaves for 10 seconds each until just crisp.

9 Turn out the "toads" and arrange them on serving plates or a tray. Spoon a dollop of the applesauce into the center of each toad, then finish each with caramelized onions and a crisp-fried sage leaf.

Why do supermarkets go crazy packaging cheese selections at Christmas time? Because this time of year is all about indulgence. I do like to indulge in a cheese board with a glass of port, but I choose the cheeses I like and, as ever, I love to add my own twist. Family and friends always giggle at me when I make "Cheesy Presents"—I know most of them wouldn't have the patience. But these delights rate too highly on cuteness charts to be left out!

Cheesy Presents

MAKES 1
PREP 20 mins, plus chilling

1 teaspoon finely chopped fresh dill or ½ teaspoon dried dill
¼ teaspoon garlic powder
1 red bell pepper, half finely diced, half reserved for decoration
1 scallion, the white finely diced, the green reserved for garnish
salt and black pepper
1 cup cream cheese
a selection of crackers, to serve

1 Mix the dill, garlic powder, diced red bell pepper, diced white scallion, and salt and black pepper to taste into the cream cheese.

2 Line the container that the cream cheese came in with plastic wrap, then pack the cream-cheese mixture back into the container.

3 Refrigerate the cheese until 20 minutes before you are ready to serve, then place the container in the freezer for 20 minutes until firm and to make sure that it holds its shape.

4 To make the garnish, cut the reserved red bell pepper into small dice and one rectangular shape (the gift tag). Next, choose a firm section from the green part of the scallion, cut off about 2 inches, and make incisions lengthwise from the bottom of the onion to two-thirds of the way up. Place it in a bowl of iced water and the scallion should open up like a bow or a flower. Choose a few nice long green pieces and blanch them in hot water for about 10 seconds, then quench in cold water and dry. This will soften the onion and you can then use it as the string for the present.

5 Before serving, set the unwrapped block of cheese on a platter. Decorate it with the scallion leaves and bow and the red bell pepper squares and gift tag, and serve with crackers.

Although the florentine is Italian in origin, my family adopted it as if it was their natural-born child. Crunchy, fruity, nutty, chocolatey—yummy! We made them as gifts and have used semisweet, white, and milk chocolate to cover them. However, more often than not, they never made it out of the kitchen!

ANGELIC STAR FLORENTINES

MAKES 16

PREP 20 mins,
plus chilling, cooling
and setting

COOK 20–25 mins

2½ tablespoons candied cherries

1 cup slivered almonds

3 tablespoons raisins

¼ cup candied peel

2½ tablespoons candied angelica

3½ tablespoons butter

¼ cup granulated sugar

⅓ cup plus 1 tablespoon all-purpose flour

2 teaspoons light corn syrup

2 teaspoons heavy cream

3½–5½ ounces milk chocolate

1 Line two large baking sheets with nonstick parchment paper. Chop the cherries into quarters, then mix them with the almonds, raisins, candied peel, and angelica in a bowl.

2 Melt the butter with the sugar and flour in a small saucepan set over very low heat, stirring continuously. Once the butter has melted and the flour and sugar are completely mixed in, add the syrup and stir through.

3 Remove the mixture from the heat and stir in the cream. You should end up with a very thick, homogenous liquid. Add the almonds and fruit and mix thoroughly.

4 Place a star-shape cookie cutter on a prepared baking sheet. Divide the dough into 16 equal portions. Take a portion and press it into the star-shape cutter. Repeat with the remaining dough, using the cutter to shape the dough into star shapes. Place the baking sheets in the freezer for 20 minutes. Preheat the oven to 350°F.

5 Bake for 10–12 minutes, until the cookies are golden brown. Remove from the oven, let cool on the baking sheet, then transfer to a wire rack to finish cooling.

6 Break the chocolate into pieces and melt it in a heatproof bowl set over a saucepan of barely simmering water, making sure the bottom of the bowl doesn't touch the water below. Spoon a little chocolate onto the flat side of each florentine, spread it across the cookie, then let sit for about 30 minutes to harden.

Friends, family, colleagues, and clients ... the list of people I want to show thanks to at Christmas seems endless. These cookies make a perfect gift, especially if you can get your hands on a few vintage Christmas cookie tins to present them in!

PIN WHEEL cookies

MAKES 30
PREP 25 mins,
plus chilling
COOK
10–12 mins

2¼ sticks unsalted butter, softened

½ cup granulated sugar

1 teaspoon vanilla extract

¼ teaspoon salt

2 cups all-purpose flour, sifted,
plus extra for dusting

3 tablespoons unsweetened cocoa powder

1 Cream the butter and sugar together with a wooden spoon or an electric mixer until light and fluffy. Gently fold in the vanilla extract and salt. Gradually fold in the flour to form a loose, crumbly dough.

2 Turn out the dough on a lightly floured work surface and knead it for 1–2 minutes by pushing small amounts of it away from you with the heel of your hand. Divide the dough in half. Sprinkle the cocoa powder over one of the halves, then knead until it has been fully incorporated. Cover the two balls of dough with plastic wrap and refrigerate for 1 hour.

3 Remove the dough from the refrigerator and roll out each piece on a sheet of lightly floured plastic wrap to a 6¼ × 10-inch rectangle. Invert the chocolate dough onto the plain dough. Remove the plastic wrap and press the doughs firmly together. Now roll up the stack as though it were a roulade, rolling from a long edge. Cover the log and chill for 30 minutes.

4 Preheat the oven to 350°F. Line a baking sheet with nonstick parchment paper. Using a very sharp knife, cut the log into thirty ¼-inch slices. Put these on the prepared baking sheet and bake for 10–12 minutes. Let the cookies cool on the baking sheet for a couple of minutes before gently placing on a wire rack to cool completely.

If you want to show off, make some of these checker cookies. They are a little fussy to make, but Christmas is all about giving, and the lucky recipient will taste your hard work 100 percent!

CHECKERBOARD COOKIES

MAKES 30

PREP 35 mins, plus chilling

COOK 10–12 mins

2¼ sticks unsalted butter, softened

½ cup granulated sugar

1 teaspoon vanilla extract

¼ teaspoon salt

2 cups all-purpose flour, sifted, plus extra for dusting

3 tablespoons unsweetened cocoa powder

1 extra large egg

1 Cream the butter and sugar together with a wooden spoon or an electric mixer until light and fluffy. Fold in the vanilla extract and salt. Gradually fold in the flour to form a loose, crumbly dough.

2 Turn out the dough onto a lightly floured work surface and knead it for 1–2 minutes. Divide the dough in half. Sprinkle the cocoa powder over one of the halves, then knead until it has been fully incorporated. Cover the two balls of dough with plastic wrap and chill in the refrigerator for 1 hour.

3 Remove the dough from the refrigerator and place each piece of dough between two sheets of plastic wrap. Using a rolling pin, roll each piece of dough into a 3 × 6-inch rectangle that's about ½ inch thick. Using a sharp knife and a ruler, slice each rectangle into five 5/8-inch-wide strips.

4 Whisk the egg with 1 tablespoon water. Put a sheet of plastic wrap on your work surface. Put three dough strips on it, alternating between white and brown strips. Brush the tops and between the strips with egg wash, then press them together. Repeat, stacking three strips above the first to form second and third layers, alternating colors in a checkerboard pattern. You will be left with one dough strip; roll it out thinly and wrap it around the log. Wrap the log in plastic wrap. Chill for 30 minutes in the refrigerator or for 15 minutes in the freezer.

5 Preheat the oven to 350°F. Line a baking sheet with nonstick parchment paper. Slice each log into fifteen ¼-inch slices. Place the cookie slices on the prepared baking sheet and bake for 10–12 minutes. Let cool for 2 minutes before transferring to a wire rack to cool completely.

These soft, gooey truffles are gloriously festive. Truffles are orthodox at all our family events, and Christmas allows us to go boozy with them. My festive list includes orange liqueur, Irish cream, brandy, and whiskey, and if you are feeling really lazy, the supermarkets sell creams with them in, so you just add chocolate! Ho ho ho! Yum Yum Yum.

SNOWMEN RUM & CHOCOLATE TRUFFLES

MAKES 6

PREP 30 mins, plus chilling

CHILL 1–1½ hours

⅔ cup heavy cream

pat of unsalted butter

6 ounces good-quality semisweet chocolate, broken into small pieces

pinch of sea salt

1 tablespoon rum, or to taste

3 cups flaked dried coconut

2 ounces marzipan

few drops of orange food coloring

24 raisins

1 Heat the cream in a saucepan set over medium heat until nearly boiling. As soon as tiny bubbles start to appear, add the butter. When it has melted, pour the mixture over the chocolate pieces in a bowl, whisking as you work, so that the chocolate melts slowly. Add the salt and the rum to the mixture.

2 Once the chocolate has melted and the mixture is smooth, pour it into a glass bowl and chill in the refrigerator for 1 hour, until it is firm enough to shape but not too solid.

3 Sprinkle the dried coconut over a large, clean work surface. Using a teaspoon, take a scoop of chocolate from the bowl and shape it into a ball using your palms, then roll the ball in the coconut until covered. Continue until you have 18 balls. To assemble the snowmen's bodies, skewer one ball with a toothpick, then repeat with two more balls to make a stack of three balls. Repeat with the remaining balls until you have six snowmen.

4 To make the noses, combine the marzipan with orange food coloring. Shape the marzipan into six little hook-shape noses, then press these onto the snowmen's faces. Use two raisins for eyes and two for buttons on each snowman. Put the snowmen on a baking sheet, plate, or tray and chill in the refrigerator for at least 30 minutes. Remove 30 minutes before serving.

Christmas would not be complete without a dessert made with dried fruits and spices. Christmas cake started out as plum porridge to line the stomach after a day of fasting and evolved over time into today's version, apparently with the help of wise men that brought over exciting Eastern spices. My nan's a wise old woman, so I stole her recipe!

CHRISTMAS Ball

SERVES 14

PREP 40 mins, plus soaking and cooling

COOK 2¾ hours

1 cup candied cherries

2 cups dried currants

⅔ cup dried pineapple

⅔ cup raisins

1 cup candied peel

1 cup dry red wine

1 stick butter, softened, plus extra for greasing

¾ cup granulated sugar

4 eggs

1 cup molasses

1 teaspoon baking soda

2 teaspoons ground cinnamon

½ teaspoon ground cloves

½ teaspoon ground nutmeg

1 teaspoon vanilla extract

1⅔ cups chopped walnuts

3⅔ cups all-purpose flour, sifted

To decorate

1 stick butter, softened

¾ cup confectioners' sugar

grated rind of 1 orange

6 kumquats, thinly sliced

¾ cup granulated sugar

about 2 cups Christmas berries (we used red currants, but you can use cranberries, only for decoration)

1 In a large bowl, soak the candied and dried fruits and peel in the wine for 1 hour. Preheat the oven to 300°F. Grease the two halves of a 6-inch spherical cake mold.

2 Cream the butter and sugar together with a wooden spoon or an electric mixer until light and fluffy, then gradually stir in the eggs. Beat until smooth, then set aside. In small bowl, combine the molasses and baking soda and beat this into the butter mixture. Add the cinnamon, cloves, nutmeg, and vanilla extract. Mix well with a large wooden spoon, then set aside the batter.

3 In a small bowl, combine the walnuts with 1 tablespoon of the flour. Stir these into the fruit-and-wine mixture until well combined. Add to the butter-and-spice mixture and mix well.

4 Gradually stir in the remaining flour. Divide the batter between the two halves of the prepared cake mold and bake for 15 minutes. Continue baking at 275°F for 2¼ hours, until a toothpick inserted into the cake comes out clean. Let the cake stand for 10 minutes, then remove it from the mold and let it cool on a wire rack. Once it is cool, cut it in half horizontally into two layers.

5 To make the decoration, combine the softened butter and confectioners' sugar until smooth. Mix in the orange rind and set aside. Place the sliced kumquats in a saucepan with the granulated sugar and ½ cup water and cook over low heat until they are lightly caramelized and the liquid is syrupy.

6 To assemble, spread the buttercream between the two layers of the cake and sandwich together. Place the kumquats on the cake over the frosting and brush the entire cake with the kumquat cooking syrup. Decorate the bottom and top with red berries.

Eggnog was as much a part of our family Christmas as, let's say, our cat. In my earliest memories, my brother and I are knocking it back to our hearts' content (I'm pretty sure now that my dad must have reduced the alcohol content). Although it's possible to buy eggnog already made, the extra effort is well worth it for a lighter, tastier, tantalizing creamy explosion!

WHITE CHRISTMAS EGGNOG

SERVES 6

PREP 10 mins, plus cooling and chilling

COOK 10 mins

4 extra-large eggs

2 extra-large egg yolks

½ cup granulated sugar

2½ cups whole milk

1½ teaspoons vanilla extract

¾ cup golden rum

½ cup bourbon

¼ teaspoon freshly grated nutmeg, plus extra to decorate

1 cup heavy whipping cream

1 tablespoon confectioners' sugar

red currants, to decorate (optional)

1 In a large bowl, whisk together the eggs, egg yolks, and granulated sugar until smooth. Pour the mixture into a large, heavy saucepan. Gradually stir in the milk, blending well. Heat the mixture slowly over very low heat, stirring continuously until it reaches 160–170°F on a candy thermometer. If you don't have a candy thermometer, you should cook the custard until it is thick enough to coat the back of a spoon (if you draw your finger across the custard on the back of the spoon, the line you make should remain distinct).

2 Pour the custard through a fine-meshed strainer into a large bowl. Stir in the vanilla extract, rum, bourbon, and nutmeg. Let the mixture cool, then cover with plastic wrap and refrigerate for at least 3 hours or for up to 1 day until cold.

3 Just before serving, whip the cream to soft peaks, beating in the confectioners' sugar as you work. Gently fold the whipped cream into the custard mixture until incorporated.

4 Pour the eggnog into glasses and decorate with a little grated nutmeg and red currants, if using.

This delicious hot spiced tea screams "drink me"! It celebrates all the amazing flavors we expect to taste at Christmas and provides a fantastic light alternative and accompaniment to everything. I love to serve it up in jars topped with my homemade Christmas Jar Toppers (see page 151) with spices and fruits on show in the jar to elevate the taste buds and provide visual delight!

Hot Spiced Tea

SERVES 6

PREP 5 mins, plus steeping

COOK 10 mins

1 cinnamon stick

6 allspice berries

3 cloves

4 tea bags

½ cup demerara or other raw sugar

½ cup cranberry juice

¼ cup orange juice

1 tablespoon lemon juice

6 tablespoons cranberries

1 Place the cinnamon stick, allspice, and cloves on a double thickness of cheesecloth. Bring up the corners of the cloth and tie them with a length of string to form a bag around the spices.

2 Place 4 cups water and the spice bag in a large saucepan and bring to a boil. Take the pan off the heat and add the tea bags. Cover the pan and let the mixture steep for 5 minutes. Discard the tea and spice bags. Stir in the sugar until dissolved. Add the juices and heat through. Place 1 tablespoon of the cranberries into each of six jars and pour the hot tea over them. Serve immediately.

Bucket Bunting

How to Make
a Bucket Chain

This decoration will need a little time to make, but it can be used as an advent calender every year. You can put anything you want in the cute buckets, covering the contents with scrunched-up gold tissue paper to keep it a surprise.

YOU WILL NEED

✂ access to a photocopier, computer, and printer ✂ paper scissors ✂ 24 miniature tin buckets ✂ 24 chosen images for buckets ✂ 25 sheets 8½ × 11-inch plain paper ✂ pencil ✂ glue gun ✂ 1 or 2 sheets colored card stock ✂ 5 feet metal link chain (available in home-improvement stores) ✂ 24 large jump rings (³/₈ inch or larger) ✂ flat-nose pliers ✂ treats of your choice

1 To make decorative covers for the buckets, photocopy and cut out the template opposite and wrap it around a bucket to check it for size. Resize it as necessary to fit your buckets. Find images you like online and print them on plain paper at sizes that work with your template. Place your template on top of the printed image, draw around the template, and cut the bucket cover out. Taking a cover, bend it around a bucket, gluing as you work with a glue gun.

2 For the advent-calendar days, photocopy and cut out the numbered labels on the opposite page and stick them to your buckets as shown in the picture. For a nice neat finish to your buckets, you can cut out ¹/₈-inch-wide strips of colored card stock and glue one around the bottom of each bucket. Let dry.

3 Now attach the buckets to the chain. For a 5-foot long chain, space the buckets about 2½ inches apart. (For chains of a different length, divide the length by 24 to establish the spacing.) Bend each jump ring open and shut with the pliers, joining a link of chain and a bucket handle each time. Now hang your bunting over the fireplace or around the tree and fill with treats of your choice.

DAY 1 DAY 7 DAY 13 DAY 19

DAY 2 DAY 8 DAY 14 DAY 20

DAY 3 DAY 9 DAY 15 DAY 21

DAY 4 DAY 10 DAY 16 DAY 22

DAY 5 DAY 11 DAY 17 DAY 23

DAY 6 DAY 12 DAY 18 DAY 24

BUCKET COVER
TEMPLATE

CHRISTMAS TEA PARTY

295

HOW TO CREATE A SEQUIN SNOOD

Christmas is the time to go for full-on Hollywood glamour with your hair, and if you're looking for a practical fuss-free hairstyle that still looks beautiful, let us introduce you to the snood! This nifty headgear has been around since medieval times and was very popular in the 1940s. It is half cap, half hairnet, is usually pinned at the top of the crown, gathering the length of the hair, and works wonders when you haven't time to do the back of your hair. Just a few customizations can transform it into an eye-catching hair accessory that exudes vintage glamour. The snood can be dressed up or down. Try adding sequins, flowers, ribbons—whatever you like. Make it truly festive with shades of red, gold, and green. Styling the front of your hair into victory rolls or elaborate curls will take it from daytime to glam evening wear.

YOU WILL NEED

✎ hair mousse ✎ tail comb ✎ heated rollers ✎ section clips ✎ bristle brush ✎ bobby pins and hairpins ✎ snood of your choice (available in pharmacies) ✎ hairspray

△ **STEP 1** Curl and set your hair in heated rollers. This style needs a lot of volume at the front, so start applying the rollers at the hairline and work your way backward (instead of working downward in horizontal sections). Keep the rollers in while your hair cools.

△ **STEP 2** Take out the back rollers and section this area off with clips while you work on the front.

△ **STEP 3** Remove the rollers from the front of the hair and divide this into three sections by parting your hair above each eyebrow. Gently tease the side sections, then smooth with a bristle brush and create a victory roll (*see page 220–21*) on each side.

◁ **STEP 4** Add the snood, pinning it at the crown using bobby pins as close to your own hair color as possible. Turn your attention to the front section. To make a curled quiff, sweep the curls back off the face with your hands and pin in place. (The rollers would have created the volume needed to do this.) Spray liberally with hairspray.

VINTAGE PATISSERIE THANK YOU

93 Feet East For allowing me to host my parties at your amazing venue, which allowed me to grow my business! www.93feeteast.co.uk

Ariotek For being the best web-hosting company I've ever come across. Drew and Collin, you are both amazing! ariotek.co.uk

Barnett Lawson Trimmings For being the only haberdashery I'll ever need. London is worth a visit just for you. www.bltrimmings.com

Beauty Seen PR Michelle, you are an amazing businesswoman. Thank you for supporting us, both as a client, and as a REVLON sponsor! We adore you! www.beautyseenpr.com

Benefit Cosmetics For making the Big Beautiful Eyes product. www.benefitcosmetics.com

Benjamin Spriggs Thank you for your support and for always thinking of me! www.thesundaytimes.co.uk/sto/public/style/?CMP=KNGvccp1-style+magazine

Bethan Soanes For being stunning and for being there for The Vintage Patisserie everytime we need you! www.bethan-soanes.co.uk

Beyond Retro For being a one-stop shop for all things vintage, and for being the place from which most of my wardrobe originates! www.beyondretro.com

Carolyn Whitehorne For support, encouragement and advice. www.toniandguy.com

Cass Stainton For getting me, and for throwing some pretty amazing parties!

Cate at Bitch Buzz Darlin', I love your energy, ambition, drive and humour – I'm a FAN! www.bitchbuzz.com

Charlotte Grace Figg Thank you for being part of the team and always bringing new energy every time I see you. I always smile when I am in your company. www.thefollymixtures.co.uk

Ciara Kate Callaghan For having amazing energy, for doing some writing and research for book one and for being the cutest thing ever!

Cliff Fluet For becoming my friend, for support, for encouragement and for understanding what I want to achieve. Cliff, you are amazing. www.lewissilkin.com

Company Magazine For support, always. www.company.co.uk

Dandy Dan You are a true gentleman. I know you work in-house now, but I still want that coffee we talked about!

David Carter For being a loyal eccentric dandy. Your creativeness has no limits. P.S. I think I did sell more books than you, no? :-) www.alacarter.com

Deborah Meaden For believing in me and providing me with a stepping stone to grow my business. It's been lovely seeing you this year and I always feel so proud when telling you about my achievements. Thank you. www.deborahmeaden.com

Denise Bates For being so supportive, incredibly fair and proud!

Denhams Broadcast & Digital To Jill (for being a little mental) and Grace. For believing. www.denhams.tv

Eleanor Maxfield For commissioning the first book and for totally getting the second book! For being by my side and supporting me every step of the way. You believe, you care and you are always fair. That totally rhymes! So happy you have become my friend. It's been beyond amazing.

Elnett Hairspray What would we do without you? www.loreal-paris.co.uk

Emma Perris For the wonderful massages you give, for support and for being my mate! emmaperris.co.uk

Fleur Britten For being fabulous and supportive. It was lovely to see you as a beautiful mum! www.fleurbritten.moonfruit.com

Fleur de Guerre For being a gorgeous and talented lady. For jumping in when I have needed you, and for being a good friend. Please stop being so fabulous! www.diaryofavintagegirl.com

Fraser Doherty and Anthony McGinley For being business inspirations; I'm always so proud to say you are my friends! www.superjam.co.uk

Grazia For support. www.graziadaily.co.uk

Harper's Bazaar For support. www.harpersbazaar.com

Hazel Holtham For being an amazing businesswoman and friend. Hazel, you are a beauty inside and out and it's been a joy watching your business develop, and even more of a joy to watch you fall in love! www.ragandbow.com

John Moore For training me when I was 18, for helping at every step of the way, for caring and being a true friend. www.rsmtenon.com

Karen Baker For creating a wealth of press that only a person who cares and is driven could achieve! You do the work of a team and I could not ask for more. Thank you for being so wonderful. It's been lovely seeing you fall in love and your eyes twinkle!

Kathy at Past Perfect For having a brilliant company that sells amazing music! www.pastperfect.com

Katie, Poppy and Richard For being the first to make a real business out of vintage. You are the leader OH KATIE! For being my friend and inspiring me. Thanks for supporting. Lets take over the world ;-) www.whatkatiedid.com

Lady Luck (AKA El Nino and Tomoko) For being the first Vintage Dance Club in London and both being so fabulous. www.ladyluckclub.co.uk

Laura Fyfe and Maura Cook Laura, you're talented, hard-working and a really nice and fair person. I could not have asked for a better home economist. You totally got the project and I hope I get to work with you again. Maura, thank you for your amazing energy and for being such a great spirit to have around. Laura is lucky to have you as a sidekick! laurafyfe.tumblr.com

Laura Cherry For being such a beauty, inside and out. You are an inspiring, hard-working lady and I'm proud that you are achieving your dream. Thank you for being part of the team.

Lauren Craig For caring about where your flowers come from, for being so talented and for being my friend. www.thinkingflowers.org.uk

Lauren Mittell For continued hard work and support! You have allowed this year to happen for me. You're gorgeous inside and out and I look forward to seeing you achieve your dreams.

Leanne Bryan Thank you for caring and being so gentle and calming. I could not ask for more from an editor! I missed all your questions on this book asking me what this and that meant! That either means I'm getting better at writing, or you understand my weirdness more!

Lian Hirst For having the best Fashion PR label in town. Thank you for understanding and supporting and being an amazing friend. I can't tell you how proud I am of what you have achieved! www.tracepublicity.com

Linton at The Fox For allowing me to host my parties at The Fox, which helped me to grow my business. And for nothing ever being any trouble; Linton, you are amazing. www.thefoxpublichouse.co.uk

Lipstick & Curls For your inspiring hairstyles and for being amazingly talented. www.lipstickandcurls.net

Louis Roederer Champagne James, I would like to thank you for making the launch of our first book so special. Thank you for believing in the brand and allowing us to have copius amounts of the best Champagne we have ever tasted (and that was unanimous!). www.champagne-roederer.com/en/

M·A·C Cosmetics For creating the perfect look. What would a girl do without her Ruby Woo! www.maccosmetics.com/index.tmpl

Margaret at Vintage Heaven Margaret! You are the most amazing woman that roams the planet! Your positivity fills my heart. Thank you for having the most fabulous business and for filling in the gaps in the book. I truly love you! In fact I want to be you! vintageheaven.co.uk

Mehmet at Can Supermarket Thank you for everything!

Naomi and Vintage Secrets For your support and for your love of all things vintage. www.vintagesecret.com

Nina Butkovich-Budden Oh Nina! Leader of the vintage hair pack! You are so talented, I could watch you work for hours. Thank you for styling the hair for the New Year chapter. A.M.A.Z.I.N.G! www.ninashairparlour.com

Octopus Publishing Group team For all being so lovely and for believing in this book! www.octopusbooks.co.uk

Patrick at Value My Stuff For being inspiring and having such a great business. www.valuemystuff.com

Peter and Sasha For always bringing amazing life to every party! I wish I could have you more!

Pete Katsiaounis For doing the illustrations for all my websites. You go beyond the call of duty. www.inkandmanners.com

Rob Davies For having an amazing business and being a friend. Your energy and support always make me smile. Thank you. www.tracepublicity.com

Rokit Thank you for being the first vintage shop I ever bought anything in! Imogen Excell, they are lucky to have you. www.rokit.co.uk

Rosie Alia Johnson For being a beautiful spirit and part of the team, for bringing the first clothes collection to life! You are a very talented beauty. www.rosiealia.blogspot.co.uk

Sales at Octopus Publishing Group Becs, Kevin, Siobhan, Terry, Vanessa… Sales! Thank you for getting the book out into the big wide world! You do me proud and I know you talk about the book with passion. Thank you!

Sarah Keen For being so bloody "ON IT". I love working with you, and having you as my crafty Girl Friday on this book was amazing. You did a stunning job. Thank you.

Sharon Trickett For being incredibly hard-working and talented and utterly fabulous. It's been lovely watching you grow Minnie Moons. www.minniemoons.com

Simone Hadfield Thank you for your hard work and kindness always… Not to mention your beauty! www.miss-turnstiles.blogspot.co.uk

Sophia Hunt, Belladonna Beauty Parlour Thank you for creating the fabulous hairstyles throughout this book. I'm so proud and happy you were part of the team. You are an incredibly talented lady and I wish you luck in whatever your future holds.

Sophie Laurimore For being a very supportive agent and for understanding my life. It's been great growing our businesses together. Thanks to you and your family for being in my Christmas chapter! www.factualmanagement.com

Stylist For support. www.stylist.co.uk

Susie and the Luna & Curious team Susie, your creativity inspires me. I must see this in everything I do now. Thank you for bringing the Luna & Curious people together and for your 24/7 support! www.lunaandcurious.blogspot.com

Time Out London For continued support.

Top Shelf Jazz Always there to perform a treat! Thank you for always being amazing at everything I have booked you for. www.topshelfjazz.com

Uncle Roy's For selling edible flowers (roses) and having the most fabulous company. www.uncleroys.co.uk

Vicki and MJ Thank you for always having so much sweet vintage style and having the best sweet shop in London (world?) www.suckandchew.co.uk

Wella Hair For making the best hair products. www.wella.com

Yasia Williams-Leedham For so much I don't know where to begin. Firstly, for your dedication and hard work. For your love of this project. For understanding what I want in your sleep! I don't think I could work with anyone else (well, I wouldn't want to, for sure!). I love you YW!

Yuki Sugiura For caring and for being so talented and creative. Work is not meant to be this much fun! You understand exactly how my mind works and together we are a great team. Your food photography makes me smile like a Cheshire cat. www.yukisugiura.com

Zippos Circus Thank you for lending us your fabulous circus equipment. You brought the children's tea party to life! When I visited your headquarters, it was one of the most special days I've had in a long time. Not only are you an incredibly amazing circus but your academy and library were breathtaking. I love that you are not precious about the amazing props you hire out to make people's parties special. Thank you for letting me into your world. www.zipposcircus.co.uk

Angel Adoree THANK you

Adele Mildred Thank you darlin' for being an inspiring creative beauty. I'm lucky to have you illustrate the book and thank you for caring that it's perfect. You are a darlin' friend and I can't wait to celebrate your wedding with you!

Alison Coward Thank you for being so proud and supporting me every step of the way.

Andreya Triana It's been a joy seeing you fall in love this year! Thank you for filling my life with music and love and endless praise! If I could sing I'd ask for a voice like yours.

Bobby Nicholls and Lord Ian You will always be my best party boys… I just need to party more! Please can we make this happen? Bobby, I love you! It's been amazing watching you grow into the King of Creatives!

Christina Lau I always feel very emotional when I need to express my thank yous to you. Thank you for your love and continued belief in me, for teaching me how to bake, and for helping with websites and business problems. You are my friend and my mentor, and one of the few people I can turn to for help. I love you darlin'.

Darren Whelan My oldest friend. Thank you for your love and support, and for reminding me to stop every now and again! Congratulations on your new life! I'm so happy for you. You and Kelly will be the best parents to your princess Nahla.

David Edwards You are my dearest friend, the perfect gentleman and a creative wizard. Your bread-making is a bit ropey, but none of us are perfect :-). Thank you for your endless support and stunning photography. I love you! And I can't wait to celebrate your wedding with you!

Dick Stawbridge I fell in love with you because you make me so happy. You make me laugh (often with bad humour), you care more than anyone I have ever met, you give so much and you inspire me with your energy, positivity and intelligence but, most importantly, with your pork-belly-making skills.

Elizabeth Osbourne Thank you for caring and teaching me to read. Your memory has never been forgotten.

Fred and Katja Künzi For taking me out of London and giving me the best memories I could wish for.

Gaia Facchini (Mouthful O' Jam) You slipped into our lives and it's like you were always here. Thank you.

Gary Nurse What a pleasure it's been seeing you be a sensational father. I'm so proud of you. Thank you for your friendship and support, and for knowing me well enough to always have a right answer in a crisis! Not only are you a handsome gent, but the beauty goes much deeper and I love you so much for this.

Gossica Anichebe For making me laugh, and for your love and friendship. Thank you.

Grandma, Nan and the rest of the ladies in my family For your constant love and kindness, and for being so proud of my achievements. I love you all.

Helen Carter For supporting me and believing in me… and for coming to my rescue!

Jake Telford and family For being the best sax player and my favourite ginger.

Jim Walker For living at the end of garden! For being my dearest friend. For your love and support, and for your proudness. I love you.

John, Julie and Katie Walker My second family! Thank you for the love you send me from all the way over the pond… Not to mention for taking me around all the vintage shops every time I came to visit!

Joseph Yianna For your friendship and support, and for being so fabulous!

Judith Biffiger For sharing your world, inspiring me with music and love, and being the gentlest, sweetest person ever!

Karen Pearson For being a friend and a business inspiration. Essex girls rule!

Kate and Joe Skully For making me laugh until my sides split, for being bloody fabulous and for the love and support you have always shown me. Kate, it was lots of fun staging your hen party!

Leah Prentice For being the second Vintage Patisserie team member. And for being my mate and causing me to laugh too many times. Mwah!

LeaLea Jones For singing like an angel, for your open heart, for knowing that hard work pays off. Ms Jones, you are an inspiration to me and your peers around you. Hackney is a lucky place.

Lee and Fiona Behan Life's a pitch and I'll never forget it! Thank you for inspiring and supporting me!

Leo Chadburn I'll always remember how we met. I was sitting in a bar with my feet on the table and you approached me and said "Your shoes are fabulous. Would you like to party?" I'm not quite sure if that's how it happened, but that's what I'll go with! Thirteen years of friendship and I love you so much. Your mum was proud of what an amazing son she has.

Mel Patel For being my mate and the only DJ I'd ever employ.

Mum and Dad For allowing me to be me. For showing me how to be open. For showing me how to love and give unconditionally. I'm the person I am because of you both. I know you tell me how proud you are of me, but I am proud of you both, too.

Natasha For your love and support.

Paul, Grandad and the rest of the men in my family For the love and kindness you've always shown me. Thank you.

Sarah, Leroy, Henry and Oscar The panda dress is getting closer! Thank you for going beyond the call of friendship and believing in me. Sarah, it's lovely to see you being such an amazing mum. I'm so proud you are my mate!

Seymour Nurse When I see your name, I smile. Your kind words live in my heart and I'll love you forever, Peter Pan!

Taj Cambridge It's been a hell of a year, babes! Every day we take a step closer towards our dream. I love you, I'm so proud of what you have achieved this year and my heart is made warm seeing you smile more than ever.

Tate and Anthony You two love birds are so inspiring with your business ventures! I love being around you and learning new stuff! www.anytodo.com is genius and that's purely because of you both.

The Strawbridges It's worrying that I feel so at home with you because you are all wonderfully crazy! Thank you for making me feel part of the family. I love you all.

Val and Co at the Palm Tree For giving me the best nights of my life and for being such a lovely family.

Vicki, Young, Rosy and Theo For your love and support, and for the party years! It's been amazing watching you grow as a family and I'm proud to be your friend.

Special thanks go to all the beautiful people who modelled for the book.

A gesture of kindness and support will never go without recognition in my world. Thank you for buying this book, thank you to the companies that have sold my book and thank you for reading my thank yous. I hope that I get to meet you one day and that you see how happy you have made me.

~

PICTURE CREDITS